Daughter, ARISE

Yvonne Ellis

Daughter, ARISE

A Journey From Devastation to Restoration

TATE PUBLISHING & *Enterprises*

Published by Tate Publishing & Enterprises, LLC
127 E. Trade Center Terrace | Mustang, Oklahoma 73064 USA
1.888.361.9473 | www.tatepublishing.com

Tate Publishing is committed to excellence in the publishing industry. The company reflects the philosophy established by the founders, based on Psalm 68:11,
"The Lord gave the word and great was the company of those who published it."

Cover design by April Marciszewski
Interior design by Nathan Harmony
Author photo by Yasmin Khalique

Published in the United States of America

ISBN: 978-1-61346-181-5
1. Religion / Christian Life / Personal Growth
2. Biography & Autobiography / Personal Memoirs
11.06.27

Dedication

To my darling husband: We have been through some trying times in our marriage, but what was meant to destroy us only served to make our love stronger. Your love and belief in me have been invaluable, and I love you more than I can ever express. Thank you for showing me how a real man loves a real woman.

My darling girls: This book is a beginning of a legacy for you, and being your mother has drawn a love out of me that I never knew existed. Especially my firstborn, no matter where you are in your life, I will always love you.

Acknowledgments

First of all, I just want to thank my Lord and Saviour, Jesus Christ, for giving me life and loving me even when I have not loved myself. He has showed me that happiness is possible if you reach out and get it. Even in my darkest times of feeling alone in this world, Jesus has and continues to walk with me daily.

Jon, Liz, Llewellyn, Carol, Len, Rose, Janet, Pauline, Frank, Gloria, Lorna, and everybody who supported me at Beulah Family Church—thank you all for your prayers, love, and guidance over the years, especially during the hard times. At Beulah, I came to learn and experience God's powerful love, and no matter where I go, Beulah will always be my first spiritual home.

Ejay, it has been a long walk for us since leaving government state care eighteen years ago, but look at us now! No longer rough girls lost without an identity, because now our identity is in Christ Jesus. Thank you for helping me to focus on the purpose for which I was called. I love you.

Sims, I love you so much; you are like a sister to me. When I wrote this book, you were always on my mind, and known that what God has done for me, he will also do for you too. Thank you for sticking with me through the bad times.

My sister, Jennifer, and brother, Jason: You have been hard on me at times, but I know it was only for my good to challenge me to a higher place in God. Thank you for fighting in my corner and for your prayers and support.

Mummy Robinson, you have looked after me well since I've been with your son. I love you with all my heart.

Anthony and Ria, thank you for all your support over the years.

Ije, thank you for your constant encouragement and words of kindness. I appreciate it.

Katherine Emmanuel, you were the one person I could rely on in my childhood. Your love for me started off this long process in my healing. Thank you.

Michelle Thomas, my big sis, I love you so much. At a time when I had no one and nothing, you took me under your wing and cared for me in my sadness. I am forever grateful to you.

Catherine, you are such a blessing in my life, and I have learned so much from you spiritually. You are a wonderful friend.

Chanel, when I was in the midst of the storm for all those early years, you prayed for me.

Pamela, Davinia, Desmond, and Deshauna, you guys were great to me when I needed the love of a family. God bless you.

And to Vanessa Grossett, my fellow author at Tate and friend, thank you for helping me to gain the confidence to finish writing this book.

Contents

Foreword

Smile with pride; that is what I do every time I listen to Yvonne describe how she is handling life's circumstances. This story is not about a life that has arrived at some fanciful place of perfection enabling Yvonne to look down on others; it is more about the strength she has received through past difficulties that enables her to live life today while being confident of the future. This is the story of God's amazing grace!

I met Yvonne through my wife's introduction at Beulah Family Church, where I have been one of three elders for over fifteen years. My wife, Carol, told me about a young woman who had a great deal of issues weighing her down. The first few occasions Yvonne and I spoke, she did not explain all the details of her background, but it was clear her past was acting like a snare around her neck. The more she would try to break free, the more her past tightened its grip. There were no illusions in my thinking; Yvonne needed more than just the power of positive thought or a few instructive words from me. So this is where my involvement started. First, getting Yvonne to trust in the Lord Jesus with her whole heart and not to lean on her own understanding of what she thought her future would turn out to be. Then for her to trust people. Stephen, her husband, and other names mentioned in this book began to be a support network of friends that loved her. We all took time to pray with her, encourage her, listen to her, and just be there for her. Slowly, Yvonne obeyed the voice of her Saviour: 'Arise, my daughter; arise.'

This book will inspire you. It is not meant to get back at or show bitterness towards anything or anyone. There are points in the book that are edgy just because of the subject matter, but it points to new hope that can be found in Jesus Christ, her Saviour guide, and inspiration. It shows how accepting God's view of herself is a means of living a life of freedom.

—Llewellyn Richards, Elder, Beulah Family Church

Preface

I don't think I will ever understand myself. All I know is through God's mercy and grace, I have come this far. The fact is I'm blessed whether I feel or even realize that I am. Many days I've sat in work and smiled at people, but inside I was a complete wreck because of the internal and external struggles I continued to face.

So many times I have felt like giving up on life, and there are still days I find hard, but I have not given up so far because something inside refuses to let me. I believe it is the strength God has given me to face every crisis I have had in my life that helps me to overcome. All my life I searched to find the piece of my being I believed was taken from me during the sexual abuse I endured during my childhood. I tried finding it in many different things—relationships, drugs, sex—but my search was fruitless and left me with low self-esteem, feeling betrayed and disappointed. I was convinced that finding what was taken from me in childhood would be the key to happiness. I believed if I searched hard enough, I would find the identity I lost then.

Only recently have I come to accept that what I will never gain back is the innocence of my childhood before the abuse happened. But I have gained a new wholeness, a feeling of completeness within my soul and spirit, which has begun in the relationship I have found in the forgiving and encompassing love of Jesus. Being a survivor of sexual abuse is one of the hardest and most painful things I've had to deal with in my life.

It was not so much the memories it left me with, although they plagued me for many years; it was the insecurities that abuse left behind. I felt worthless and suffered from low self-esteem. It is only in the last four years that I have learned to start liking myself again. I did not feel worthy of anyone's love, let alone God's, and felt I was only good enough to be used by other people. I often wondered if my life would have turned out differently if I had the inner resources to put boundaries in place sooner. As you read my book, you will see I have been through many heartbreaking situations and faced many trials, and if you are someone who has been through one or all of them, I want you to know that you are someone of great worth in God's eyes. I want you to know that there is still hope despite your situation, whatever it may be. I hope you will understand that despite the despair and hurt I have faced, life can still turn out promising. God has come to heal the brokenhearted and to set captives free.

My Childhood

Our family was normal enough. There was my brother, Darren, who was the most hyperactive out of the three of us, and he always sucked his tongue. He was cheeky and loved to tease me and my sister about the way Mum plaited our hair, the clothes we wore, or basically anything he could use against us as ammunition. My sister, Janet, addicted to sucking her thumb, was happiest when she had a pocketful of biscuits. Out of the three of us, she was the quietest, which made her an easy target for us at times. Then there was me, Yvonne Nicole White, the oldest child, born August 19, 1976, in St. Thomas Hospital, who could be shy at times but was mainly loud. I was the family joker, making everyone laugh at times with my jokes and zany personality.

I grew up on Winstandley estate in Battersea and enjoyed living there, as I had many friends. For the first four years of my life, we all lived in my nan's house at Holiday Square, which was across the way. It was cramped, as me and my siblings shared a room. Then our parents got their own home on the next block, Fowler Close. It was a three-bedroom house like my nan's, on the top landing. It did not have a garden but had a playground downstairs, which we could see when we stepped out our front door onto the balcony.

Mum was a beautiful woman who always looked immaculate and kept our home looking immaculate too. She could be funny at times, and I have vivid memories of her singing nursery rhymes to us. Mum was good at everything she turned her hand to; I remember her teaching me how to knit.

Then there was my dad, who was twenty years older than Mum and who dressed out of date. He had these horrible sheepskin jackets from the seventies that he always wore to work or when he went out to the pub or bookies. Mum would complain and say he was old-fashioned, but you could see he thought he was fashion forward when he put them on. Dad was happiest watching cricket or down at the bookies on a Saturday afternoon. The other person who made up our family was my nan, who never went out much, apart from going to Brixton market or Northcote Road food shopping. She spent most of her time peering through her net curtains. Some of our friends on the estate nicknamed her "Peeping Thumbelina" and "Neighbourhood Watch," as she spent so much time at her window. We teased her about her curtain habits, but no one messed with her. On a couple of occasions she chased after certain kids who started trouble with my brother, shouting after them in her native language Jamaican Patois. She worked as a sewing machinist most of her life and when she came to England, worked different factory jobs until she reached her sixties.

We came from a large family with relatives as far as Jamaica, America, and even England, but there was no relationship with any of them. In fact, apart from meeting some of them once at a family party, we did not know who most of them were.

At Christmas I would always be the first one up dancing when Dad put on reggae music, and these were the times I remember being happiest. Every Christmas Darren, Janet, and I would get up around five o'clock in the morning and sneak downstairs to sit by the lit-up tree, shaking our presents to guess what was inside. Darren always wanted a remote control car or a transformer, and my sister and I would want a Barbie or Rainbow Brite doll that we could dress up with accessories. We never had the guts to open the presents before time, and we did not have to wait long to find out what we got—well, no more than a few hours, as my mum would hear us and tell us to go back to bed. A few hours is a long time to a child, but when we finally opened our presents, we all got what we wanted—one main present plus small ones each. It was great playing with our toys while watching Christmas cartoons that came on the telly. Christmas breakfast was always my favourite meal of the day: fried plantain, baked beans with the onions fried in it, gammon, and hardough bread. Mum was a great cook, and she made amazing cakes and dinners, even doing inventive things with ice cream by adding raisins and a tiny bit of rum to make it more interesting. There was nothing she cooked that I hated—except liver; liver was the only piece of food I would discard under the dinner table.

My mother seemed lonely at times, and her world only revolved around my dad. No friends rang the house for her, and she never had any friends around. The only person who came round was my nan, who would have to talk to Mum on the doorstep, as she was not allowed in except for at Christmas, when Dad invited her around. They did not have a good relationship.

Mum a good parent, as she installed into us some of the important life skills we needed to get through life, such tidying up after ourselves, being clean, and looking presentable, but I don't remember her ever making a habit of saying she loved me or giving me reassurance that I was worth so much to her or helping me to develop a sense of self-worth. I remember her singing nursery rhymes when I was young, but in the later years—seven onwards—it stopped. But in spite of that, I admired her and wanted to grow up to be just like her—smart and beautiful. Mum was like superwoman in my eyes. She worked as a bookkeeper and was good at math and spelling and took care of the family finances and looked after us, cooking every day. Dad, on the other hand, could just about write his name. For all of Dad's showcasing and showing off, he was not as intelligent as Mum and relied on her tremendously to manage his business accounts, as he had trouble reading and writing.

Dad had his own business as a painter and decorator, and you would know when he was in from work, as the smell of white spirit and turpentine filled the house. He sometimes worked long hours, and on the days he was home, he would spend the day watching cricket or be down at the betting shop across the estate.

He did not play games with us often, but I have memories of the three of us trying to tag team Dad and jumping on his back and laughing. At times I felt like his favourite, because he always laughed at my jokes the most. But there was another side to him that was more prominent that I did not like. Dad had a very bad temper and would get angry over silly things, and his answer to any problem with my sister, brother, and me was to beat us.

When it came time for my beatings, I would go upstairs before he got home and pray that Mum would not tell him what I had done or that if he knew, he would forget, but he never did. So I would end up putting on several layers of clothes so my skin would not get many welts. When he beat me, I felt like he enjoyed it too much. I could see it in his eyes. I was fearful of him; we all were. When he came home in a bad mood, which was often, everyone would be on tenterhooks. Fear was definitely evident in our house. If things were not going right for him, he would vent the brunt of his frustration on Mum in a vindictive, soul-crushing way by making cruel remarks.

We had a large dining table in our dining room, and Dad's favourite chair was at the head of table; he never sat with the chair not pulled fully in. One day Mum, who, instead of asking him to pull in the chair so she could get past (she did not want to upset him further, as he was in a bad mood), tried to squeeze past. He took this as an opportunity to tell her she was fat and needed to lose weight. She was clearly upset. All he had to do was pull the chair in, but it was all about control and making her feel insecure.

Another time, Mum wanted a change of hairstyle, so she had it cut. When she came back, she was happy about her hairstyle and was expecting compliments from Dad, but he went mad and started cussing and carrying on, having a go at her. Then, shockingly, he took her back down the hairdressers to have a go at the stylist about the cut. It never occurred to him that she wanted a change of hairstyle, as many women do in their life. He thought it must have been done against her will. He was very controlling, and to him, Mum was a piece of property that he owned. Every decision that was made in our family revolved around him. What was weird was that she was upset for a short while then would go twice as much out of her way to please him.

Mum always made sure that before he came home the house was immaculate and his food was exactly how he wanted it, as there were plenty of times if it was not to his standard, he was vocal and rude. She even made sure that his favourite special brew or Tenant beer was cold in the fridge. Mum did this every day. Despite being tired from holding down a full-time job, she came home and behaved like his slave. I hated the smell of his favourite beers because they had a pungent smell when he opened it, which wafted around the whole room. When he drank he was mellower, and coupled together with his smoking, he was not as agitated. He smoked so many Golden Virginia roll ups, his forefinger had turned brown.

They were never an openly affectionate couple who kissed and cuddled, apart from Christmas time when they would have a dance to *Lover's Rock*. Dad's way of being affectionate to Mum was making sure she had a nice showpiece home that was decorated nicely. The furniture in our front room was all mahogany, and in the eighties, mahogany was the furniture to have if you wanted to look like you had money. They had arguments, which they thought we could not hear, about money. Dad liked spending his money on gold jewellery, like bracelets and sovereign rings, which, worn all at the same time, looked extremely tacky. He would only wear them on a Sunday when he went to his meetings in the countryside. He had expensive tastes, and when he bought a BMW car, that was the icing on his cake. Every Sunday, with the hosepipe dangling out of the kitchen window, Dad would be outside washing and polishing it like no one's business. It was always a bit nerving when we had family outings, as when we were in his car, we were not allowed to eat or drink in it and had to be very careful about the way we closed his precious car doors. If we slammed them too hard, he would shout.

In dealing with any trouble between my brother, sister, and me, he believed if two of us were telling the truth, the other one was lying, so they would end up getting the beating. This opened the way for us to manipulate this stupid rule, and we regularly put it into effect. One day when our parents were out, my brother and I were doing something that definitely was a no go in the living room: throwing cushions. I got a bit overexcited and threw the cushion with all my might at my brother, who ducked, so it ended up smashing our mum's expensive porcelain lamp to pieces. Crying hysterically, I tried to glue it back together, but it was no use and I knew I would get a beating. My little sister was singing in my ear that I was going to get in trouble and to wait until dad found out. Because I did not want a beating, I begged and begged my brother to say our sister did it. He agreed, in exchange for sweets or something silly like that, so the two who were lying blamed the one that was telling the truth.

All hell broke loose when they arrived home. Mum was upset her lamp was broken, and Dad was ranting and raving, grilling us about who was to blame, so we executed the plan, and Sister got the licks. I'm not proud of what I did, but at the time in our family, it was a normal thing to do. It was never fair, but Mum never questioned him; what he said stood.

At dinner times he did not like us talking or laughing at the table, so most of the time, we ate our dinners in silence, but we, being kids, would muck about kicking each other under the table or pull funny faces when he was not looking. One of us would end up laughing, and this would start a chain reaction, which resulted in us being ordered off the table. We took great joy in slyly winding him up in this way after a while.

Joseph Tritton Primary School represented, for me, a great source of happiness in my childhood. I loved being at school because I could just be myself without feeling anxious. My favourite classes were rounders, cooking, or crafts.

I liked a couple of boys in school but never had a boyfriend, as I was too shy for that. Dad warned me and my sister that even having boys as friends was not acceptable. That never really bothered me, as crushes from afar were much nicer. I loved school trips, especially swimming, even though I was an average swimmer. On a school trip to Butlins in Wales, I nearly drowned swimming in one of those pools that in an instant went from the shallow end to the deep end. Frantically splashing and beating away at the water, I started going under. If it was not for a girl named Lisa who came to my rescue, I would have been dead. She was one of only a few children in my class who could swim in the deep end unattended, as she was a strong swimmer. From what I was told, Lisa dragged me to the side of the pool and then the lifeguard jumped in, dragged me out, and pumped my chest. All I remember was coming to with water coming out of my nose and mouth and a very bad burning sensation in my head. That was the first time in my life I had a conscious feeling of death and life. I did not want to die, and although life at home was far from happy, my life was not that bad after all. That episode was over as quickly as it started, but I did not get back in the pool that day. The rest of the school journey was brilliant, and I was thankful that my parents paid for and allowed me to go, as other children, for whatever reason, could not.

When I was somewhere between nine and ten years old and was becoming more aware of life, I craved time with my mum and wanted her to spend special time with me. Sometimes she gave me a hug, but I felt at times that she was distant. She always looked more at ease with my sister. Maybe because I was oldest, I felt not as loved, but then again, my brother, being the middle sibling and the only boy, did not get much time either.

I had a good relationship with my siblings in between our petty childhood disagreements, and on weekends we would go across the estate to our nan's house and cause havoc by jumping on her sofas and doing the things that were forbidden at home. We liked winding her up and eating all her biscuits and crisps. We then would go and play outside with all the other kids.

Living on an estate was cool, as there was so much going on. Fights, dancing games, bombing up and down hills on chopper bikes, skates, and skateboards, we would play for hours—games like "knock down Ginger" and water bomb fights, if it was hot. If it was a Saturday evening, all the kids would go in early evening to watch the *A-Team*. We never missed an episode, and we even had the *A-Team* sweaters. Every child on our block had one. If you did not have one, you were not cool. This was what weekends consisted of, and I loved it. The eighties were a cool era to grow up in. Hot summers, ice lollies, and skating about, knocking for friends—that's what life was all about. As long as I had that outlet, I was okay. Our friends were never allowed over our house, not even in the passageway by the front door, and we were not allowed in their houses, which made us feel left out among the other kids, as they were allowed inside each other's houses.

One Monday morning in the summer of 1985, I did not want to go to school, so I lied to my mum and said I was sick, thinking she would stay and take care of me. But she could not stay home, as she had to go to work. Dad overheard this and said I could stay home with him instead. It felt strange being home without my brother and sister, as they were usually there. But I soon forgot about them as I got comfortable on the sofa to watch cartoons on the TV. I was disappointed Mum could not stay with me, but the deed was done now, as I had lied to stay at home.

Above the racket of the TV, which was loud, I could hear my dad calling me from bed upstairs, so I ran up to see what he wanted. I thought he was calling me to wash dishes or run to the shops. As I knocked and entered, he was still in bed. He told me to get into the bed. Standing there in my yellow Tom and Jerry vest and knickers set, I asked him why. Dad had never invited me into their bed before, and he did not answer my question. Instead, he firmly asked me again. I got in the bed, which was so big I felt it would swallow me up; he was completely naked under the sheets. Panic and fear gripped me, and I felt immediately something was wrong. I started to cry. He put me on top of him and rubbed himself on me, whispering to me with his terrible morning breath that I was a good girl. I was shaking so much and so shocked that I thought I would pass out. Desperately looking for an excuse, I told him I needed to go to the toilet. Only then he let me go.

If anybody would have told me at the time that the girl I once was would be gone forever that day, I never would have believed them. But all of a sudden, I found myself facing a whole new dimension of feelings that were alien to me. He tried to reassure me that he was doing something good, but I felt anything but good. I felt vulnerable, shocked, scared, and confused. When I got to the bathroom, I locked the door. All that kept running through my mind was, *He is going to hurt me*. I kept trying to understand what had just happened, if it had happened, or if I was dreaming. I zoned out, and all my thoughts seemed go in slow motion.

After sitting on the bathroom floor for what seemed like an eternity, I could not figure out what to do next but knew I had no choice but to face whatever was to come my way. Fortunately, when I came out, he did not make me get back in the bed. Dad told me not to tell anyone and that it was our secret. I did not understand and did not even know what he had done. Anyway, why would I want to share something so awful and shameful like this? Why could I not have a nice secret to share with him, like giving me extra sweets or a pound note without my brother and sister knowing ? You know, the type of secrets you see the daddies do on TV. Thoughts like these went through my mind as I looked at my dad and nodded, trying to stop the hot tears from overflowing out of my eyes. I went into my bedroom, got under the sheets, and cried so much my eyes stung. Up until that point in my life, I was able to cope with some of the strange things that made up this family. Like every time mum combed our hair, instead of putting it in the bin, she kept bagfuls and bagfuls of our hair, from the day we were born, stockpiled in the bottom of our wardrobe. Or at times my sister, brother, and I had a bath; it consisted of a strange-smelling, blue liquid. Dad would cut the seats out of our knickers, which were returned with them missing. I learned to cope with the secrecy and the unexplained questions to so many things, but I could not cope with this. I felt it was my fault because if only I had not lied to get off school, I would not be in this mess.

For the reminder of the day, I kept myself as invisible as possible. First thing I did when he was downstairs was had a very good wash, following the usual routine of leaving my used knickers in the bucket, as he always took them. Then I stayed in my room. My brother and sister got home, and I felt awkward.

Mum arrived home and asked me how I was, to which I replied I was fine. I didn't feel I could tell her what happened, as we didn't have that type of relationship. Anyway, what would I say? I did not even have a name for what happened and felt she would not believe me. Dad acted fully normal and gave no indication to what had happened only a few hours before. He did not act or look like he had anything to hide. In fact, he seemed happy, while I struggled to keep myself together. My whole world as I knew it had come to an end.

Life carried on as normal for everyone else, but for me, life was never the same again. I went from being a relatively happy child who ran around the house in her vest and knickers to a girl who made sure at all times I had clothes on, locking doors behind me wherever I could. I became moody and withdrawn and could not see the happiness in anything. Inside my head, everything was bleak. The jokey, playful Yvonne had gone, and a new Yvonne was born—an angry, sad, and hateful girl who hated her life. When I looked at my dad, hatred came over me for what he had done, yet I knew hating him would not change the situation. It wasn't as though I could do anything about it or go anywhere else. This family was all I knew, and Dad was in control of this family.

It is amazing how in the midst of trauma, the body and mind adapt to cope with unexpected situations, and with no one to turn to or a shoulder to cry on, I dealt with it on my own. But all I wanted was my mum to tell me it would all be okay. I believed it was just one nasty experience that would never happen again, but I was very much mistaken.

Dad, eager to finish what he had started, the very next evening, as I got washed in the bathroom, knocked on the door and asked to be let in. I did not want to let him in, and tears came to my eyes for a second. Then, remembering that there was no other way out of this, a different, stronger side to me took over. There was no time for tears. No matter how scared I was, quickly I opened the door, as Dad was not a person who liked to be kept waiting, and you never made him ask you anything twice. Dad sat on the edge of the bath while I stood by the sink, internally shaking. He informed me that from now on when I washed in the evening, I was to call him. He never told me why, but I found out soon enough anyway.

He told me to open my legs. Then he proceeded to force his finger in my vagina then turned me around so he could look in my bum; then he quickly left. Embarrassment and humiliation left me rooted to the spot in this small bathroom, which now became a prison of suffocation. I felt ill and trapped, slowly losing my mind. I wanted to cry but knew if I did, I would be in trouble, as my brother and sister would want to know what was wrong. It was not like the day before, when I was at home by myself and could cry. When I opened the bathroom door, I saw my mum sitting on her bed, watching TV. She didn't look my way, and I know she saw me, as the bathroom was right opposite her room. I desperately wanted her to look at me, to look into my eyes and see that something was wrong. Was there no suspicion as to why her partner, my dad, was in the bathroom with me? It was like I was invisible.

It was bedtime, so I got into the double bed I shared with my sister. Lying there in the darkness, a sense of hopelessness washed over me. What had happened to my life? All of a sudden, I was a stranger in my own home. No longer did I fit in, and I could not share with anyone what was going on. I tried to think if I had done something bad that had made him treat me this way. I knew my brother and sister were not getting this treatment. How I longed for Mum to make it stop. My sister slept peacefully beside me, life's routine still the same for her. I thought Dad would feel guilty or bad seeing how uncomfortable I was, but he didn't. The bathroom episode was the start of my new routine every night, and just as I got used to that, by the end of the week, more was to come.

It is not nice feeling that any day fear will kill you, but since these horrible encounters had started, I got used to the feeling. Every time afternoon came at school, dreaded fear would grip me and I would get painful bellyaches that would last all the way until after my evening wash, when he would come into the bathroom to do his check. The bellyaches continued until after the weekend had passed.

I will never forget the first time my dad came into my room late on a Friday night. My sister and I had been in bed since ten o'clock, and Dad was not in, as he was down the pub. We hardly saw Dad before we went to bed on a Friday, and to be honest, I was glad. So imagine how startled I was to be awoken by him hovering over me in the dark. Fear had entered the room. I knew it was late. To say I was startled is an understatement. In a low enough voice that my sister could not hear, but low and close enough for me to smell his alcohol and tobacco-stained breath, he told me to get up, put my clothes on, and wait underneath the living room stairs for him to come and get me. I hid and waited under the stairs, scared and insignificant, like a dirty rat under a sewer. I waited for what seemed like an eternity. Part of me was getting impatient, wanting to get whatever that was going to happen to me over with, but another part wanted anyone in my family to come down and find me there.

When Dad eventually came down, he told me to put on my coat. I looked up at the clock that hung on our living room wall as the front door opened; it was after midnight. All the lights were off in our house, and as he opened the front door, bright orange streetlamps from the estate greeted me. In a strange way, I found them comforting after being under those dark stairs for so long. We walked along the balcony; Dad walked about ten paces in front of me, and I walked obediently behind him like a dog trailing behind its owner. A couple of times I tried to talk to him, but he told me to be quiet. We went down the stairs and proceeded to walk round the back of the estate near my nan's house. The route did not make any sense, and I thought I was not going to see my family again. We eventually ended up by the back stairs to my nan's house, but why was I there? Maybe Nan wanted me to come and stay over, as she lived in a huge three-bedroom house by herself. She must have been lonely. Apart from the time we spent as family living with her when I was small, we had never stayed over her house. We got to the set of stairs that led to her door. Dad told me to wait under the stairs and to be quiet. I knew then that Nan had not wanted me to stay over.

I was freezing waiting under those stairs. All I had on was my green cotton nightdress with a pair of jogging bottoms underneath and some shoes on. At least I was not left in the dark, as these stairs were lit. I did not have to wait as long either, as Dad came and got me quickly.

Nan's house was completely dark. We went upstairs, and Dad told me to wait to one side near the ladder that went on to the roof of the house so if Nan came out of her bedroom, she would not easily see me. I watched as he took out a key and opened one of the bedroom doors. He kept a room over my nan's house. which he told us was his office. Many a time when we came to see Nan on a weekend, my brother, sister, and I were always curious as to what he kept in the room, because it was always locked. While snooping around we would look through the keyhole to try to see what he kept in there. Now that I was going to find out, I did not want to know.

The room looked like a cosy little bed-sit decorated light blue, and it smelled of incense. A couple of pictures hung on the wall—one of them was Jesus. In the picture he had long, flowing hair. His arms were outstretched in a welcoming gesture in a long, flowing, white robe. A couple of shelves on the wall housed weird ornaments, and a half-round table had zodiac-type gold symbols painted on it. Then directly under the shelves, a longer table cover with a white tablecloth had a couple of candle holders, an open Bible, and other objects on it. A blue sofa bed had been folded out with sheets laid on it, and he even had a TV, VCR, and a little fridge.

The room was not as sinister as I had imagined, but most of the objects were weird and very cold. Suddenly, after being silent for so long, Dad became friendly and talkative as he beckoned me over toward his mahogany desk, which had two cans of Coca-Cola and two packets of Golden Wonder crisps he had brought for me. He then lay on the sofa bed and asked me about general things like school and my friends, which he never would do. Nervously, I sipped my coke and ate my crisps as I tried to squeeze myself into the chair jammed firmly between the desk and the wall, as the sofa bed was laid out, dominating most of the space left in the room. Dad kept asking if I had nearly finished my crisps. I said no, sensing something bad was going to happen again. I began to be really chatty. My belly ached, and every part of my being inside panicked. I needed to buy myself more time, and the only thing I could use, as I had done before, was the need to go to the toilet. He was not happy that I asked but said okay. Peering around the door, he gestured for me to go quickly.

I sat on the closed toilet seat in the dark and cried, for I knew where this night was heading. I did not want this and kept wondering what I could do to make it stop. I wondered if I begged and cried to him if he would he feel guilty and remember I was his daughter.

But I knew there was nothing I could do. My voice would not be heard; I had no power. I was just a child.

When I went back into the room, Dad was now under the sheets naked. Knowing there were no more excuses, he told me to take off my clothes and get in the bed with him. I had to listen to him tell me about my mother and his problems, like why he didn't like sleeping with her or why he didn't like sleeping in the same bed as her when she was on her period. It made me extremely uncomfortable, as he was talking about my mother in a way that I could not relate to and I had no idea really what he was talking about. I knew I had to be brave because there was no escape from this nightmare, which was now part of my life. He treated me like I was his lover, not his daughter, and at no point was concerned that he was hurting my small body, only caring about his own disgusting needs. A different side came out to help cope, the side that had to be brave and not show emotion, even though inside I was drowning in an ocean of tears.

He was very heavy, and my chest and ribs hurt under his weight. He did things to me I cannot even describe. He would say, time after time, that I needed to get used to it and if I relaxed, it would be easier for him. As strange as it sounds, looking back, maybe in the midst of this horrible experience, God was looking out for me by not allowing this. After he finished he gave me a tissue to wipe myself up and hurried me to get dressed. Then it was back on the cold and what seemed like a very long walk home. I was not allowed to get washed and had to stay reminded of what happened until the next morning when I could have a proper wash.

I will never forget the first time my so-called father crossed the boundary of what was meant to be a normal father and daughter relationship, something that was my natural right. I will never forget that first time over at my nan's house, a place for me that was part of those Saturdays when I played out and had fun summers. He destroyed my childhood.

Every Friday and Saturday night from the age of nine to thirteen, it was part of my life. I tried every manipulative thing in my power to stop it happening, even going to bed extra early so that when he saw I was sleeping he would leave me alone. I would pretend to be asleep but would hear the bedroom door sliding over the carpet. It never stopped him. He would wake me up and tell me it was time to go. Day in, day out, the same old routine continued with him sneaking me out of the house, invading my space, and interfering with me. I was like a pendulum—one minute loud and naughty, the next withdrawn and quiet. I found it hard to be around my friends and felt as though I did not belong. My mother did not seem to notice or care, as she was caught up in running the home and pleasing him. Never once did she comment on the fact that I seemed different.

One hot summer's day when I was ten years old, I sat on the floor outside my house, the hot concrete burning the back of my legs. Days like this were always a joy to me because I loved playing out in the sun . Usually I'd have my skates on or be playing some kind of game with my friends. I cannot explain what happened; it was like this black feeling suddenly came over me.

Crazy, sad thoughts crashed around in my mind, so I decided I would kill myself. I went upstairs into the bathroom cabinet and took out three Paracetamol tablets and swallowed them. Being young, I did not realise I needed to take many more tablets for it to have any effect. I went downstairs to the kitchen and told Mum what I had done as she stood over the sink washing dishes. Her response was one of rejection; she told me to go outside and play and not to be silly. I was so angry with her. I only wanted her to notice what was happening to me. You would think if your ten-year-old child had told you they had taken tablets, whether it was true or not, you would be concerned, because why would they come out with something like that? I was depressed and wanted someone to rescue me from what I was going through, but in that moment, I really wanted to die.

Some weekends my mother allowed me to go up to the pound shop up at Clapham Junction, as I was old enough to be responsible. That was not the proper name of the shop, but I called it the pound shop, as everything was so cheap. It sold stuff like funky-coloured pens, Filofaxes, stickers, and lots of bright, colourful things.

I didn't get much pocket money and had only about fifty pence on me. When I got in the shop, there were so many things I wanted but had not enough money, and I saw a pen I liked. An overwhelming urge came over me to take the pen. I knew it was wrong to steal, but I tried justifying why I should steal this pen. I made up my mind; I wanted it. Carefully I looked around to see if anyone was watching me in the round, magnified mirror that was at the end of the aisle. With the coast clear, I sneakily put the pen up my shirt and walked out as simple as that. My heart was excitedly beating so fast inside my chest, and a rush of guilt and excitement come over me at the same time. Taking the pen without being caught made me feel good and far outweighed any feelings of guilt. When I got back home, I went upstairs and proudly took out my prize. That day, the love affair with stealing started. Sometimes if Mum saw me with something she had not seen before, she would ask where I got it from. We were not allowed to borrow stuff from other children, so I would lie and say it was a present instead. I became a good liar and was very sneaky. Sometimes my brother or sister would have to come with me, not out of choice, but because Mum said we had to stick together whilst playing outside. Every time, I came away from that same shop with something I could not afford. I encouraged my brother to do it, but he was scared, but I convinced my sister to carry a Filofax for me once.

My stealing was not confined to the pound shop and began to surface at home. While Mum was at work, I would go through her wardrobe and take out her jewellery to wear to school. And when she came home from work and put her bag down, I would sneak upstairs, go in her purse, and take money out. I felt bad stealing from her, but not enough to stop me. When Dad left his trousers lying around, I would go in his pockets and take money from them, as they were always good for plenty of change. I never felt bad about stealing from him.

Stealing made me feel alive, and it was something I had control of, because my own body was certainly not mine. Knowing what consequences would happen if they found out was not enough to stop me; I chose to keep on doing it. The twenty and fifty pences I stole soon became pound notes. Dad didn't notice, but Mum did, and she no longer left her purse in her handbag. I found out her new hiding place, at the top of her wardrobe. One evening after dinner, with my family downstairs, I told Mum I was going toilet but instead went to their bedroom, stood on top of her makeup chair, and opened the top of her wardrobe. Hidden well, under her clothes, I found her purse and took out three one-pound notes. Just as I was getting down from the chair, my nan opened the door and caught me. Nan started shouting, "What do you think you're doing," and before I could tell a lie, Dad burst through the door and started hitting me with his belt, cursing me and saying I was bad news. The pain from the belt was nothing compared to the pain I felt inside. Seeing his face contorted with anger and disgust confirmed what I already knew: he hated me.

My behaviour got worse, and I could not be trusted, as I stole and told lies about everything. Even the twenty pence I used to tell my mum was for Brownies to put in the charity tin, I would take and spend nineteen pence on penny sweets and put a penny in the tin. At Brownies I was quite disruptive and jealous of the girls who earned badges that were sewn down their sleeve from being good and completing tasks Brown Owl (that was the Brownie leader's name) had set them. Every week after we had games, Brown Owl would congratulate them and tell them what good citizens they would grow up to be. I would tease and mock them, calling them Goody Two-shoes and other names. But secretly I wanted people, especially my parents, to be pleased about me and Mum to sew my badges on. But for some reason, I was never good enough.

As the abuse continued, I thought if I just did the things Dad wanted me to do during it and even pretended to enjoy it, he would see I was a good girl and love me the way I wanted to be loved. But even when I forced my soul to try, he treated me no differently in the week. He was still the same—bad tempered and always moaning. No praise or encouragement, just negative vibes.

I was kicked out of Brownies because Brown Owl said I was disruptive. I was only upset because it was an hour more that I had to spend in my house. Ironic, really, that I left Brownies with one badge for the one thing Mum did a lot of at home: housecleaning.

There were never any surprises in my parents' relationship, until one day out of the blue, Mum came downstairs crying. When we asked why, she told us Dad was leaving. I remember the look on my brother and sister's faces, one of excitement and relief. I was excited but apprehensive at the same time and would only believe he was actually leaving when I saw him, with my own eyes, walking out the door with all his belongings. For a moment my imagination ran wild, wondering how much nicer life would be with the four of us as a family, how much happier we would all feel. I felt bad for my mum, as she loved him, but my happiness was far more important, and I did not care how selfish that was. We listened intently on the stairs for any type of information, and from what I gathered, the reason he was leaving was because she had not met up to his impossible standards. We could hear him opening and closing doors inside the room. Then suddenly the bedroom door opened.

We quickly tried to resume our original positions at the bottom of the stairs, but as we were doing this, Mum called for me. Puzzled, I looked at my siblings and went upstairs. On entering I was greeted by the sight of Dad packing his stuff into a suitcase and Mum crying, begging him not to go. I was shocked to see Mum in this state. Although I had seen her cry, the reason was never obviously clear, but now I could clearly see the reason: Dad. Dad looked directly at me and told me he wanted to take me with him, but I just wanted to scream in his face that I hated him. He had been the source of all the pain and unhappiness in our family but was oblivious to the misery he caused. So I answered no and told him I wanted to say with Mum. He asked again, this time in a calmer, gentler voice, but it made no difference to me, and I defiantly told him no. I left the room to the sound of Mum crying and Dad having a go at her.

I walked back downstairs to my brother and sister and told them what happened. They were puzzled and asked why Dad only wanted to take me. I stood quietly, not knowing what to say, then angrily replied that I did not know why he wanted to take only me. The thought of having to spend another day with him made angry.

Some time later Mum came down, followed by Dad. With no tears, shouting, or drama, she announced he was staying. My brother, sister, and I reflected upon the sadness in each other's eyes, but it was nothing compared to the desperation and sadness in my heart, as my only opportunity to be free was now gone. My brother and sister looked at me like it was my fault for not going, but there was no way I would have ever gone with him. If they knew why, maybe they would have understood.

Life at home continued the same, with Mum doing her usual routine of working, cooking, and cleaning and Dad working, going down the betting shop on a Saturday, drinking, and having outbursts of temper. I would hear him be rude to Mum and often wondered why she put up with him; it was not as if she was ugly. She was an attractive woman in her thirties with the potential to achieve anything she set her mind to. She reminded me of a beautiful bird that had lived in a cage its entire life, but when she had the opportunity to spread her wings to fly out of the cage because the door was opened, she would not. Dad represented that closed cage door, with his constant negativity. She wasn't physically kept prisoner, but mentally, she let him keep her as one. He was a controlling and constrictive sixty-year-old man who only cared about what made him happy. He was never completely faithful to Mum and had been unfaithful at least once, which she knew about and accepted. They looked odd together, and because of the age gap, you would be forgiven for thinking they were not in a relationship.

I wondered obsessively about why she would choose to stay with him and did not believe it was for our benefit. In our world we were sad and fearful most of the time. When I looked at Mum, I could see her sadness, but still she chose to remain. I became a very anxious person because of the abuse and began to believe I was always sick. It was first triggered by the tummy aches I got when evening wash times and weekends came and permanently seemed to be there. Apart from always being sore and in pain in the vaginal area, I did not display any other pain or physical symptoms of an actual illness, but I was convinced I was dying. These feelings I carried right through my early twenties, and I believe they were birthed from the sadness I could not convey that I carried inside. I wanted to believe I was ill because then it would justify and make sense of what I felt. I wanted to go back to before the abuse began, when I was a vibrant and fun girl. I knew that playful and loving Yvonne was gone, replaced with a young girl lost in confusion and despair.

Walking home from school one day, I saw my friend Glen on my balcony. I often saw him near my house, as he was good friends with my next-door neighbour's son. I stopped to talk to him for a while about school, and we were giggling about silly stuff. I was never really that confident having one-on-one chats with boys and only felt confident talking to boys when I was around my friends. I started to become aware of the time and knew Dad was home early, as I saw his van, so I kept looking down the balcony stairs, feeling a little awkward and scared because if Dad caught me talking to boys, I would be in trouble. Glen started telling me how much he liked me and started getting a little too close for comfort. Suddenly he pinned me to the balcony with one arm across my chest, using the other hand to force his way into my knickers. He really hurt me. I was begging him to stop, but he would not listen, so I screamed. On hearing me, our friend Luke, the next-door neighbour, came out of the house. But instead of helping me, as I was on my knees, clutching my private parts, crying, he just laughed as they both ran back inside his house. I limped into my house, crying, and told Dad what happened. He went ballistic, ran outside in his slippers, and banged down Luke's front door. Luke would not open it, so my dad shouted obscenities through his letter box and warned Glen if he ever touched me again, he would kill him. Needless to say, he never touched me again after that day. In a way I felt Dad must have loved me to react like that, but on the other hand, I was more upset because he was doing much worse than Glen had done. It left me feeling confused. This incident confirmed a belief in me: I attracted this kind of behaviour, and I soon let myself become a target for any male to touch me how they wanted.

After dinner one evening—I was around eleven at the time—I went to use the toilet and was greeted by the sight of a lot blood. It looked like I had been stabbed. I screamed for my mum and thought this was the evidence that I, in fact, was dying, but I was confused as to why I had never bled like this before. She came upstairs into the toilet, and I asked her why I was bleeding. She told me I had started my period. I tried to ask questions about what a period was, and she became irritated, went out of the toilet, and returned with a pad for me to put in my knickers. There was no explaining why it happened or any kind of talk about what it meant for me.

Still, that was to be expected in my family. Everything was secretive; nothing ever openly discussed. I found out through playground talk and a teacher at school that it happened to all females once a month for a very long time. I got used to it after a few months, and although they were painful, I was actually pleased when it came, as it meant Dad would leave me alone for one week a month. No bath-time checks; no late Friday or Saturday nights. Towards the end of the week, he would ask if it was finished and then when it was, the abuse would resume back as normal. The older I got, the more desperate I was to escape, but I did not know how to. I was like an animal trapped into a corner, trying to scuttle around for a hole to get out, and because I could not, I became very confrontational and aggressive toward my peers and would end up in fights. I became known for my temper and aggression, so much so that my brother would sometimes call me for backup if he got into fights with older kids. I was not shy in this sense and was like an erupted volcano when I got into a rage. I would cry and shake, and a red mist would just come over my mind. I wanted destroy anything in my path. I used these situations to vent my frustration, which I kept bottled up at home.

Mr. C was someone who was of great importance to my dad, and every Sunday, he would put on his suit, topped off with a cowboy hat and naff gold jewellery. All we knew was that a group of them, only men, would meet up somewhere in the countryside and that Mr. C guided them on how they should run their families. Nobody knew who he was or his full name; he was only referred to as Mr. C. One Sunday just before Dad was going to one of his meetings, he called me upstairs to his bedroom. Kneeling down in front of me as I sat on the bed, he looked me straight in the eyes and told me if I ever told anyone about what he was doing to me, I would become deaf and blind and I would also lose my voice. Mr. C told him to warn me that this would happen and that it was normal for dads to do these things to their daughters to prevent them from becoming pregnant when they were older. When he had finished, I went into my room, shaking and scared. I did not know how much more torment I could take. I wondered what type of powers Mr. C had to be able to make someone go deaf and blind; he must be very powerful. I could see Mr. C was a frightening influence, just because Dad did what he asked. He had nothing to fear, as I had no one to tell who would believe me about what he was doing, as I did not have a name.

Christmas 1988 was not exciting for me, and I spent much of it daydreaming in a world of my own. I remembered how I used to love the excitement of Christmas—dressing up in our best clothes, the food. It always felt like a magical day just because it was Christmas, but now it felt like another ordinary day for me. Never knowing what each day would bring, apart from the routine days of abuse and being on a constant state of alert, took its toll on me. I was in no mood to pretend to be happy and join in the festivities and after dinner went up to my room, lay on my bed, and cried. I loved the new clothes my mum brought for me to wear: a blue and white stripy sailor T-shirt and blue drawstring cord trousers. As I had started to develop breasts, I felt uncomfortable, as I did not want anymore unwanted attention from my dad. My sister came upstairs to tell me that Dad wanted to take some family pictures, but I did not, so Mum shouted for me to come downstairs. Tearfully I stood with one hand leaning on the speaker, not knowing what to do with myself with Dad taking pictures, telling me to fix my face and smile. I did not want to smile, and after a couple of Polaroids, I tried to say I did not want to take any more. My feelings counted for nothing, and I was made to feel like a drama queen, so I switched mode, as I often did, to hyperactive Yvonne with the fake smile to join in the pretentious happy family Christmas. I developed different sides to hide my secret torment. Little was I to know that Christmas 1988 would be the last I would have at Fowler Close.

Some Sunday mornings Mum and Dad would send my brother, sister, and me across the road to St. Michael's, a basic-looking church, a little run down in appearance, as the council had not invested any real money in its upkeep. Two evenings a week it served as a youth centre, and most of the kids who lived on surrounding estates would come and hang out and play snooker, table football, or just chill to music and buy stuff from the tuck shop. There were not many places like this around where I lived, so most of the kids would go to York gardens adventure playground, the basketball cage, or wobbly bridge, a small playground with swings and a bridge that was always broken, hence the name. Or if we could not be bothered, we just hung out on different parts of our estate.

St. Michael's looked very different on Sundays; gone were the pool tables. Instead, laid out in their place were rows of uncomfortable plastic grey chairs and at the front, a wooden pulpit with a Bible on it. There were never more than thirty people who came on a Sunday, and sometimes my next-door neighbours, Luke and Akemi, would come too. We only went to church to misbehave and cause trouble and because it got us out of the house. Reverend Michael would start the service by walking down the middle of the aisle holding a huge wooden cross crucifix with Jesus hanging on it, with two other vicars by the reverend's side. My neighbour Luke would try to stick his foot out to trip up Reverend Michael. I would encourage him to do it and sit and laugh my head off. We also sang really disruptively and did not take any real notice of the message Reverend Michael was giving. Part of me wanted to listen, but I had too much energy to keep still.

One afternoon, I decided to go over to my nan's house. As I walked up the stairs to her front door, I could see it was slightly ajar, so I pushed it open. I called her a couple of times, but there was no answer or sign of her downstairs, so I went upstairs. I pushed open her bedroom door and was greeted by the sight of my dad, naked, on top of my nan, who was in her nightdress in the middle of the day. Dad got up casually and got dressed as I stood there, not knowing what to make of what I had just seen.

We left my nan's house, and Dad appeared anxious. He said if I promised not to tell mum what I had seen, he would buy me anything I wanted from the sweet shop. So I promised not tell, as I filled up a carrier bag full of crisps, sweets, and more Juicy Fruit chewing gum than I knew what to do with. When I got home, my brother and sister were shocked by the amount of sweets I had and asked where I got the money to buy them from. I told them Dad paid for it. I learned more and more from incidents as these that my family was all about keeping secrets and telling lies. I learned my dad was a manipulative liar with no truth in him.

I never kept that promise and was only ever waiting for an opportunity to tell Mum what I saw because I wanted them to break up. That time came one day when she was telling me off. Angrily, I told her I saw Dad and Nan together naked in bed. At first Mum stood quietly, not saying anything, then began raising her voice to Dad. Instead of asking him if it was true, Mum said to Dad I was lying about him, about her mother and him. They called me a liar, and Dad kept asking me when I was going to stop telling lies as he removed his leather belt with the big buckle. Shaking, I defiantly stood my ground, repeating I was not lying and that it was the truth, as blows from his belt rained down on me. He continued to beat me while Mum stood by and did nothing to help me. I should have known better than to ever think that she would believe me, as, according to her, I was an attention seeker. Yet again, as with so many situations in this family, lies prevailed over truth.

A few months later in September 1987, I started secondary school but really missed primary school and all my friends. It was the only place I had any stability. Now I had to start all over again, making new friends, as all my friends were at different secondary schools. Still, at least I had my best friend, Neeta, who lived on one of the other estates not far from me, so we still saw each other regularly.

My new school was called Burntwood Girls School and, compared to primary school, was huge. I was highly nervous on my first day but soon loved it, as I made new friends quickly. I became popular with the older girls, whom I had for backup if I got into a trouble, and became popular with the rebellious girls because of my rebellious nature and willingness to do bad things for a laugh. Going to secondary school ignited a fuse in me and became another outlet where I vented my frustrations. I remember on one occasion the French teacher was just about to start the lesson but forgot some books, so she had to pop back to the staff room. I took my Bobby Brown cassette out of my walkman and put it into the cassette player on the teacher's desk. Hurriedly I sat back down, bursting with excitement about what would happen next. Everyone was sniggering. As she came back in, she gave out the handbooks, telling us the tape would explain everything. As she pressed play, Bobby Brown's song "My Prerogative" belted out. Some of us got up singing and dancing about, but the teacher went mad and asked who was responsible. I did not admit it, and even though my classmates knew it was me, no one grassed me up. Miss tried to keep the whole class back for detention during morning break, but as we were on the ground floor, a few of us decided we would ignore her and climb out of the window. I loved being disruptive.

I stepped up my rebellious attitude at home, and whenever my mum told me to do something, I would be difficult. I felt like she only interacted with me when she wanted to pick at me about something, and it aggravated me deeply. I looked up to my mum and wanted her approval, but she was too distracted to notice. I felt sorry for her, as she had a lot to put up with, but I wished she would take an interest in my life. If she had, she would have seen I was dealing with a lot of pain.

My geography homework one night was to build a replica block of flats where I lived, using paper to make the houses. I asked her for some glue, and she told me there was none and that I would have to make paste out of flour and water. When I tried to stick the little houses together and place them on my design, they would not stick and looked awful. I complained to Mum, but she said I would have to make do, so I cheekily muttered under my breath, "That's what I always have to do." Mum shouted that she was tired of my cheek and that when Dad got home I was in big trouble. That was all I needed to hear, and, as I had experienced many times before, a huge surge of anger came over me and, coupled together with a desperate need to escape, got me to my feet to run. Just hearing I would have to face Dad and have him in my space again pushed me over the edge. I only had my slippers and house clothes on; I did not even grab a coat. I just ran downstairs, opened the front door, and ran and ran. In my head I was running away from home, but I had not planned where I would go.

Running through Winstandley Estate in the dark was scary but better than staying in my house. The cold, autumn breeze stung my face, and beads of water streamed down my cheeks, but I kept running. Before I knew it, I was at the door of my friend Neeta's house on the Badric Court Estate. She looked surprised to see me out this late, as it was after nine o'clock. Nevertheless, she let me in. I was so angry and blurted out what happened with my mum and told her I did not want to go back home. Neeta asked why, and at this time did not know I was being sexually abused, so to her it seemed a trivial thing not to go back home.

I had not even been there fifteen minutes when there was a knock on Neeta's door. Her mum opened it, and I could hear my mum asking if I was there. Mum was standing in front of me telling Neeta's mum there was a misunderstanding, but Neeta's mum was concerned, as I was distressed. Looking into her eyes, I was desperate for her to see that something was really wrong and that it was not just a case of a teenager rebelling, but Mum convinced her. Resigned to the fact that my first running-away episode was now over and that I had to go back home, I got up and left with Mum. On the way back she said nothing. The closer I got back to my house, my stomach ache intensified; I knew I was in serious trouble.

Back home, I went upstairs and got into my nightdress and into bed. I heard the front door close downstairs and knew Dad was home. The suspense was unbearable, and my heart pounded hard in my chest, for I expected him to burst into my room any minute to beat me. I waited, but there was nothing. I knew Mum told him what I did, and he was not the type of person who could hold his temper if he was angry. Something was not right. I lay there awake for as long as possible until my eyelids got heavy because I was scared to go to sleep.

When I got in from school the next day, things seemed relatively normal. Mum came in, cooked us dinner, and we ate. Still, nothing was said about what happened the night before. That was, until Dad came in, and immediately the whole atmosphere changed. I knew the cause of his mood, as he ushered only my brother and sister off the table and told them to go upstairs. He did not do his usual shouting. He only told me he was fed up with my behaviour and that he was going to hang me from the ceiling fitting in the top passage. I was crying, and for once Mum pleaded with him not to do it, so instead he took the flex from an old kettle and tied me to one of the dining room chairs. He tied my hands really tight behind my back then took off his leather belt and beat me. The lashes did not hurt as much anymore because I mentally zoned out and let my mind take to me to another place. I accepted there was nothing I could do to change what I had been up to this point—an object to be sexually used, a child who was irrelevant. I was only loveable to a certain age, but as I got older, I had become a hindrance. Why did they bother having me? I did not know because, according to my dad, I was liar and useless in fulfilling his needs and to Mum, the older I got, I was an attention-seeking drama queen. Still, I must not have got on her nerves that much for her not to allow him to hang me.

Finally he untied me, and I cannot remember how long I was sitting there, but by the time I got up, my bum was numb. I got up slowly, and he told me I was grounded and if I ever did anything like that again he would kill me. Those eighteen steps to my bedroom felt like I was climbing a mountain. I went straight into the bathroom and locked the door. On examining my wrists, I could see these huge grooves where the kettle flex had been tied so tight; plus, I had some other marks on my legs from the belt.

The next day I went to school, and as soon as I hit those gates, I put on my happy face and became hyperactive and overly happy.

In class form group June 1989, which we had at the beginning of each day, my teacher, Miss Smyth, informed the class we were having a special lesson. A guest speaker from a children's charity called Child Line was coming in after registration to give a talk on issues that affect some children and teenagers.

This lady spoke in a way that we could understand what she was explaining to us. It was the talk that changed my life, as I finally found a name for what my dad had been doing to me for the last five years: sexual abuse. I tried to let the words sink in, but my hyper mind had trouble registering it. She explained that sexual abuse consisted of inappropriate touching all the way up to sexual intercourse and said it was rife in countries all over the world and gave different examples of what classified as abuse. She finished her talk by telling us that if we knew anyone who was going through it or if we were experiencing it ourselves, there was a confidential, free phone helpline we could call, as she gave out leaflets. I sat there feeling paranoid, looking out of the corner of my eye, believing the other kids were looking at me knowing I was going through abuse. I finally had a name for what my father was doing; finally a name for this thing that was destroying me. I thought about what this moment would feel like for a very long time and imagined that it would free me all of a sudden. I imagined that once I had a name for the behaviour I called "thing" I would just burst out, say it, and someone would hear me and come to my rescue. Now the day had finally come, and all I could do was sit in my chair, shuffling uncomfortably, looking at this lady who had given me the keys to take the next step. Even though I now had this information, I did not know what to do with it.

The next day as I was walking home I saw my friend Neeta by the park and told her about the visit at school and that my father had been sexually abusing me for years and about the incident where he tied me to a chair with the old wire flex from the kettle. Neeta was upset by what I told her and asked me what I was going to do. I just looked at her and shrugged my shoulders.

Days passed, and on the way home from school, I passed by my nan's house to get biscuits. On leaving Nan's, I walked around the balcony and was greeted by my brother running toward me. He finally caught up to me and breathlessly told me the police were at the house asking for me and that they were searching the house, looking for the wire flex Dad tied me up with. Immediately I thought I was in more trouble and ran back round to my house with my brother. I entered the door to police searching through Dad's decorating cupboards as he was standing there. I had told Neeta where Dad put the flex when he finished tying me up with it, so they came with a search warrant to look for it. They asked Dad where it was, and he said he did not know what they talking about and that he never tied me up. Mum backed him up.

In the living room, a social worker from Wandsworth Council told me she was here with the police, as they had received information from the head of Neeta's secondary school, given by her mother, that I was being sexually abused by my dad and that they were here to take me into emergency care, pending a full investigation. I stood rooted to the spot with Mum crying in the background, my brother and sister looking bewildered and confused.

It happened so quickly that there was not enough time to take in everything that was being said. Together with another social worker, they led me upstairs to my room and closed the door. They tried to reassure me that I was not in any trouble but were deeply concerned by reports they received. One of the social workers reached on to my bed and picked up a teddy bear and asked if the bear was mine. I replied it was, and in a gentle voice, she asked me to show her, using my teddy bear, how Dad had been touching me. I tried my best to show her but ended up feeling embarrassed and ashamed. The social worker called Mum into the room and asked for a bag so I could pack some stuff. Mum gave her two plastic bags. I looked around the bedroom, trying to decide what to take, but did not know what to begin with.

How was I to decide what to bring in a few minutes when the things I had accumulated in this bedroom I shared with my sister had been the last thirteen years of my life? The social worker could see I was upset and confused as to what to take, so she gave gentle prompts on what to pack. Inside, all different emotions ran through me about leaving home—feelings of panic, sadness, and fear of the unknown, but also relief that I would be out of my dad's clutches. I never wanted him to touch me again. The time had come for me to leave, so I said bye to Mum, who by now stopped crying and grabbed my teddy. I said good-bye to my brother and sister, who hugged me so tightly, crying. She did not want me to go. Knowing I was leaving them behind was the hardest part, as life was never going to be the same for any of us ever again. I was extremely sad.

Care Years

The social worker explained I would be staying with a foster parent named Miss Stewards that night. We did not drive far, and the area was very familiar—not too far from Neeta's house. One of the social workers took my bags out of the car, and as we walked up the stairs to my new temporary home, the smell of fried chicken wafted down the hallway. Miss Stewards opened the door, and the social workers introduced us. She was not at all how I imagined a foster parent to look like, but then again, I did not know what to expect. Miss Stewards was a black Jamaican woman, quite big in stature, who spoke in a firm but friendly voice, and my first impression of her was that she was quite nice. Miss Stewards walked me and the social worker to the room I would be sharing during my stay with a girl called Rochelle. Rochelle was lying on the top bunk bed and jumped down to greet me and made me feel welcomed immediately. The social worker stayed for a while. Then she left, telling me this was only a twenty-four hour placement and that tomorrow a meeting would take place to discuss where I would be living for the foreseeable future, and on that note, she left.

Miss Stewards called me into the living room to meet her three daughters, who were all older than me, and two of them were definitely older than Rochelle. On first glance, they did not look like sisters, as they had very different features, colour tone, and shape.

The eldest was very short with light skin; the middle daughter was very tall, and the youngest was very chubby but pretty. They said hello quietly as they looked me up and down, and I could tell by the look in their eyes that they did not know what to make of me.

I had packed in such haste that the things I really needed I did not have, so Rochelle was kind enough to share her stuff with me, although she was surprised they only let me bring a couple of bags of stuff. Rochelle was seventeen years old and was really pretty and kind. You could have easily mistaken her for being older, as she was mature beyond her years in her attitude and also street smart.

The room we shared was yellow and so small that it only had space for a wardrobe, chest of draws, and a bunk bed. Rochelle slept on the top, and my bed was at the bottom. The first night was very strange, and I found it hard to sleep, as I kept thinking of my mum, brother, and sister. I was tearful, wondering what this unknown life would hold for me now, and I felt bad for my mum. I kept thinking that if she knew the real scale of everything that was going on, she would have kicked him out. Maybe now she would realize and do something about it, and then I could go back. Despite how she treated me at times, I still believed she loved me in her own way and that she would want to have me back home.

The next day, Miss Stewards woke me up to get ready because a social worker from the child protection team was coming to collect me to have a chat. It was weird waking up in a strange bed, opening my eyes to a woman who was not my mum. I was unsettled during the night, as I kept thinking my sister was in the bed because we shared a double bed at home. She would kick me with her foot and tell me I slept badly. It was going to take a long time to get used to this new life and new routine. After I had my wash, Miss Stewards showed me where the cereals were in the kitchen and explained a few house rules, which seemed straightforward enough. Maybe living with a foster parent would not be so bad after all.

I was taken to a special suite situated in a police station that was for talking to especially to children. The social worker who took me there was different from the one who brought me to Miss Stewards's the day before, and she introduced herself on her arrival at Miss Stewards's house. Straightaway, she explained that she worked with the police child protection team. In the suite were lots of teddy bears and big cushions strewn on the floor. Ionia—that was her name—sat on the cushions with me and began to talk. A microphone hung from the ceiling, and the only other feature that stood out was a big mirrored window, which I later found out was double sided. On the other side, our talk was being filmed with a psychologist who was watching. We talked about school and my friends. Then she asked about my family and relationship with my dad, more specifically about the abuse. I found it difficult to talk about, and it took me a while before I opened up about the subject. I did not cry, as I found it hard to show emotions that I had built up over the years in front of this stranger. Afterward I was taken to St. Thomas hospital for an internal examination. I had to undress and get into a flimsy little gown with nothing underneath, which made me feel vulnerable. Ionia assured me that she would be present the whole time, but that did not calm me, as the doctor was a man, which upset me. He did not do the examination straightaway and was very understanding and patient, and when he did the examination, he allowed me time to adjust myself when I needed to. At the end of his examination, he explained to the social worker, in front of me, that my hymen was badly damaged and this was a sign that sexual activity had taken place. I cried, and Ionia hugged me and told me I was going to be okay now. How I really wished it was my mum telling me.

It was long day, and I did not reach back to my foster home until late afternoon. When I arrived back, Miss Stewards was not in a good mood; she was shouting at Rochelle about something. Rochelle came into the bedroom, upset, and we could hear Miss Stewards talking to her daughters about her in a bad way, which was not nice to hear.

My twenty-four-hour stay turned into a six-month stay, and I soon became subject of her treatment too. She would say mean things about us and never made us feel like a natural part of her family. Her behaviour towards us reinforced that. She had a washing machine that fully worked but made it clear that I was expected to wash all my clothes by hand. Fair enough. If it was just knickers, I could understand, but a whole week's worth of clothes at a time? I did not even know how to hand wash clothes, but Rochelle taught me. Her daughters, however, could use the washing machine anytime they liked. Being a Jamaican household, the main food that was cooked was from the Caribbean, and I loved Caribbean food, as I was brought up on this at home. Miss Stewards would cook this type of food up for herself and daughters, while Rochelle and I had to eat anything else, which she did not prepare for us. At every turn we were treated differently, made to feel like outsiders. Rochelle taught me everything I needed to learn while I was there and took me under her wing. I will always remember the kindness and love she showed me during a confusing time in my life. I learned how to make boiled dumplings and corned beef since there was always plenty corn beef in her house. When I wanted biscuits, Rochelle gave me some of hers, as she had a little stash of supplies she brought herself. I felt intimidated coming out of the bedroom a lot of the time. If I went into the bathroom, I could hear Miss Stewards making comments to her daughters about me and laughing. The anxious knots in my stomach were present all the time, but I soon learned how to adapt while I was there, and that was to stay invisible as much as possible. I just stayed in the bedroom and only came out to eat, use the toilet, or use the bathroom, and go out to the youth club back down my estate at St. Michaels. I was there over six months and only went into her living room to sit down twice. Rochelle used to give back as good as she got when Miss Stewards's daughters started their nonsense. I began to stay out later and later so that by the time I entered her house, their little crowd in the living room would have dispersed, as she would be in bed and her daughters in their rooms.

When the social worker visited, Miss Stewards would be a completely different person—all niceness and smiles, talking about me in a positive light, but the reality was different. I was tiring of her behaviour towards me, and at one of my case review meetings, I blurted out what was going on in her house and how Rochelle and I were treated. My new social worker looked alarmed, as she thought the placement was going well, but if they saw me as regularly as they were supposed to, I would have told them sooner. Social services were clueless. I ended up with quite a few different social workers during my time in care and could not relate to them, as they definitely could not relate to me. They may have had their university degrees, but they lacked empathy, and all their work consisted of was following rules and regulations, but this did not allow for empathy and common sense. But thanks to Rochelle, who left Miss Stewards shortly before me, I learned to find my voice and speak up about things that bothered me, and boy, was I going to use it. Staying with Miss Stewards and her daughters was unbearable, and I told them exactly that. I did not want to stay in her house anymore.

My life became more and more complicated by the time I left her house in 1990. During my time there, I was kicked out of Burntwood School and Margaret Press tuition centre because of my unmanageable behaviour. I started to vent hate toward adults in authority by lashing out and being violent. I got into a lot of fights, on one occasion getting a knife from Nan's house to deal with a girl I had a fist fight with. Fortunately, she ran home, and when I buzzed her door to come down, she would not. I instigated a lot of negative behaviour because I was unhappy, and to those who were on the receiving end of it, I was a nasty person to be around. I don't know why my behaviour escalated out of control, but I guess it stemmed from the lack of boundaries being a child in care brought and the disruption of being uprooted from my family brought into my life. I would go to school with all these emotions running through me every day, feeling unloved and uncared for, trying to concentrate on school. It became too much. It had been nearly a year since I left home, and Mum had not made much effort to see or contact me. I missed my brother, sister, and friends on the estate. The fear I felt for so many years now became anger, and I hated my life. Every minute of every day, I was reminded of the pain and rejection I had experienced, because the memories would not go away. In the care system, I was just another faceless child, a case that needed to be discussed. Social services saw these files before they knew me, so I always felt pre-judged. Mum was invited to the case conferences but refused to come. She made excuses about not being able afford the fares to get there, but the truth is, even when social services offered to help, she still did not come. I was being unfairly treated by her for telling the truth in my time of need. My family turned their back on me when they knew the right thing to do. My life was a mess, and no one around me could understand the despair I was feeling. A couple of months later, I was told through my social worker that the Crown Prosecution Service could not take the case any further, as they did not have sufficient evidence to secure a conviction. The police and social workers involved tried their hardest to press the case forward, but the main evidence—the room I had been abused in—was completely cleared out. Apparently when the police turned up at my nan's house with a search warrant, the room had been stripped bare. Nan and Dad removed all carpet and furniture, including the blue sofa bed. CPS said while there was physical evidence, this alone was not enough to build a strong enough case. So I went through all of that for nothing. I was so angry when I found out. While I was at the counsellor's office, I trashed it and tried to smash a bottle over her head. Dad had got away with what he had done and lived life as normal with my family, while I suffered, left living in state care with a couple of bin bags full of clothes to my name. Where was the justice?

Patricia Davis was a woman who lived on my estate, whom I had known from a child, as her children and I went to the same primary school. She was always very nice to me, and when she heard what had happened, she looked out for me all the more. Patricia was the only adult I trusted, and I respected her. When my placement broke down at Miss Stewards's, she spoke to my social worker and offered to take me in and be my foster parent. I was over the moon initially, and the deep-rooted rejection that had taken root in my soul was relived temporarily, as I had a deep complex about being unlovable. Her gesture made me feel loveable and wanted, but after a while, little things started to chip away at me inside again, leaving me insecure, and I became deeply unhappy. Patricia did everything possible to make me feel part of her family. Her children called me their sister, and she called me her daughter. Whenever we went to see any of her family, that's how she referred to me. Living back on the estate again would be a dream come true, I thought, but I felt threatened by my father's presence and by ordinary family life. When her children got loads of presents, I expected lots too, and when it did not happen, I took it as a sign that I was not loved the same as the others and became jealous. My mind was all over the place with all my problems and with my constant need to be the centre of attention. It was only a matter of time before the placement broke down. Aunt Patricia felt unable to keep me safe with my father living in such close proximity, and it was hard for her and her children having someone like me around unsettling things. When she sat me down to tell me that I would have to go to a new placement, she was crying. I shouted at her that she did not love me, but in spite of all my verbal noise, in my heart, I knew she loved me.

I reached Falcon Grove kids' home at fourteen years old and had already started smoking cigarettes and drinking alcohol. Falcon Grove was the first children's home I was sent to and was a stone's throw from Miss Stewards's house. It was around the corner from

Shillington I.T centre, where I was now attending for education. It was a centre for children kicked out of mainstream school.

Being in a children's home was an opening in my life for all kinds of wrong behaviour. I had a curfew time of nine o'clock but constantly came in later. I would go and check my friends back on Maysoule road estate at the sports centre, and we would get someone older to buy alcohol and cigarettes for us. I would get back to the home drunk and become very confrontational with staff, as they were adults. I saw them as a threat to my existence. I never believed that when they gave me advice on my life they were it doing because they genuinely cared. I believed they were doing it for control, and I did everything in my power to do the opposite of what they asked or wanted. When they took my pocket money or privileges away, I would hit, kick, or throw plates or glasses at them. I would also threaten the other kids in the home and pick fights, which always ended with me being restrained on the floor by around three staff holding me until I calmed down. I never thought twice about my behaviour or if hitting them hurt or not. I did not take into account they were human; to me; they were just objects. I hated what they represented—authority and control—so that was a good enough reason for me to justify hitting them.

One night I was with my friends Natasha and Jasmine, chilling out and smoking cigarettes with a guy we knew, when he rolled up what looked like cigarette, but when he lit it, it smelled different from tobacco. Out of curiosity, we asked if we could try some. After sharing around a few of these roll-ups, I decided I liked it. It was called cannabis, but we called it weed, its street name. I soon became addicted to the way smoking weed made me feel, and it became a regular fixture in my life after that night. Whenever I smoked it, my problems seemed so far away, and I was a more happy and confident person. The world seemed better when I smoked. Back in the day, ten pounds was a lot of money to spend on one thing. So my friends and I would all chip in money to get a bag of weed or a draw. When

I was returning to the home, I would chew gum and try to spray my clothes to mask the smell of weed and alcohol. Cigarettes were not too much of a big thing with the staff, as most of the kids in the home smoked. They did not condone it, and if you were caught with cigarettes, they would be confiscated, as the legal age was sixteen. But being caught with weed would be serious enough for them to call the police. Those sneaky, lying ways I learned during childhood came in handy in care, and I used them to my advantage to cover up whatever I was doing that was wrong.

Falcon Grove was a lonely place, especially at night, and some nights I would cry myself to sleep only to awake after a bad dream and find I had accidently wet the bed because I was scared. Other nights, as the weed and alcohol took its effects, I would just fall into a deep sleep. I kept most of my stuff in bin bags in my room, as I never felt at home and because I never knew how long I would be staying.

Christmas came, and I spent it at Falcon Grove. My social worker tried to arrange a visit for my mum, brother, and sister to come and see me, but Dad stopped all contact. I was very angry with my mum, who, as usual, did whatever he said. I vented my anger by acting out, throwing furniture around, swearing, and shouting. I was lonely and depressed and hated Christmas. A few skeleton staff on worked the shift, probably because they wanted to do their good Christmas deed and get double wages. There were only a few of us kids that remained, the ones whose parents could not have them around, even at this time of year. Aunt Patricia was good enough to have me round over some of the Christmas holidays, which was very nice, as I had fun.

I found it hard to get up the morning after drinking and smoking, and I would try to stay in bed for as long as possible. The staff would knock my bedroom door every half hour trying to get me up for I.T centre. As I was reluctant to go, they would walk me there to make sure I attended. While I was at I.T centre, most of the time I tried to apply myself to work but would get caught up in another kid's drama. Just because I had problems did not mean I did not have my dreams. When I grew up, I wanted to be a stockbroker or a barrister. All the teachers said I was bright and intelligent for my age, but they all said I found it hard to apply myself to tasks, as I got distracted easily. The problem with me was that I liked getting into trouble and rebelling.

One day when I arrived back from I.T centre, the head of the home, along with three other staff, were waiting for me as I walked in the door. I was told I was being taken to Middlesex Lodge, a secure centre, to cool off, as my behaviour was out of control. I tried to make a run for it, but the staff caught and restrained me on the floor. My key worker was trying to tell me to calm down, but it was no good, as I was going berserk. They carried me like a barge pole and put me into one of their horrible, green Wandsworth Council vans, the same one I used to refuse to get in when they had outings, as I thought it was uncool. I did not want anybody seeing me in it, as they would ask questions.

Middlesex Lodge was, by far, the most shocking place I had ever been to since I entered the care system. Middlesex Lodge was a secure unit for teenage girls and was split between floors. The first two units called Drayton and Hayes were more moderate units, and the third, which was situated on the bottom floor, was complete lockdown, where you could not go out at all and had to be accompanied by staff at all times. I was placed in Drayton unit which was on the top floor. Middlesex Lodge was very strict, and the main doors to the building were locked at all times. You were accompanied to the shop by a member of staff, and even then you had to earn that privilege. Eventually when you could be trusted, you could go out by yourself. Pocket money had to be earned by doing chores such as cleaning floors, dishes, or toilets, amongst other things. I got on with the other girls really well, as we all had one main thing in common: being as rude or disruptive as possible. While I was there, I did not spend much time mooching around thinking of my problems, as I was trying to learn, like the others, how to beat the system. I behaved only when it suited me and did the opposite when it did not. In the daytime we went to education in the school wing, but it was a joke, as education consisted of colouring pictures for two hours at a time like the infant children do; there was no structure. PE was boring, and the teacher was scared of us, so with that level of boredom and rebellious teenage girls, it was a recipe for disaster. Certain groups of girls had arguments and fights with girls from other units, as education time was the main time they saw each other.

During one lunch break, my friend and I lied to the staff by saying we wanted to go to the sweet shop across the road, but we got a bus to Southall instead. We had a wicked time and got an older person to buy Thunderbird alcohol and cigarettes for us, and then we went and got our noses pierced. Needless to say, when we eventually returned to the lodge drunk, we were grounded for a week and only allowed to go out escorted by a member of staff.

Ambulances and police cars came to Middlesex Lodge on a near regular basis, as someone would be kicking off or trying to harm themselves. The majority of girls in Middlesex Lodge had been sexually or physically abused. Many were in a terribly bad way, and I will never forget the amount of pain and hurt I witnessed as many let their inner despair out by cutting themselves with any sharp object they could find, overdosing on Paracetamol or abusing solvents. The pocket money was not great, and the amount of going out time was not huge, so quite a few girls sneaked in spray deodorants or lighter fuel to sniff. Spray deodorants were banned because of this problem, and you were only supposed to have roll-ons, but during weekend visits to relatives or friends, some girls would sneak them in. Failing this, on visits to the shops, some would get strangers to buy solvents for them and use it before going back to the lodge. I tried it a couple of times, but I did not like the aftertaste it left in my mouth, so I stuck to smoking weed. The times I could get my hands on weed were few and far between, so my consumption of alcohol and cigarettes became more. You rarely saw the girls who were in the secure lockup unit downstairs, as they were on twenty-four-hour lockdown from the moment they arrived to, for most, the moment they left. Only on rare occasions was anyone from down there transferred to an upstairs unit. Bedtimes were strict on weekdays but more lenient on weekends.

One evening, a member of staff tried to show me up in front of my friends, who I sneaked down to see on Hayes unit. So I decided I was not going to have that, and, as she stood behind the glass panel door wounding me up, I took a flying kick into the glass, which caved in. My purpose was to get the glass to shower her in the face, but as I went to walk off, there was blood everywhere, and another member of staff screamed at me to get on the floor, as I was injured. It was only then, when I looked at the back of my ankle, that I saw a gaping, big hole with my tendons showing. I was taken to hospital to have an operation, and my leg was put in a cast for six weeks. The doctor said that the main tendon in my leg was damaged and that if it had completely snapped, I would have been walking with a limp for the rest of my life. I was scared hearing that, but still, it was not enough to make me think about my temper.

About a month later, a white girl made a racist comment to a black member of staff whom everybody liked on Drayton unit. What was said spread to Hayes unit downstairs and ended up causing a full-scale riot. But even on crutches, I still managed to find myself in the thick of it, hopping after a member of staff on one leg, beating her over the head with one of my crutches, and I smashed plenty of plates and damaged the furniture. That night resulted in around sixteen of us being arrested, fingerprinted, and charged with affray. It was claustrophobic being locked in a cell overnight, and I was cold, as I was arrested in my green Air Jordan T-shirt and green-striped boxer shorts. We tried our best to wind up the police sergeant by singing the song "Ten Green Bottles" down from a hundred, which we found hilarious. We ended up driving the sergeant mad, and he would come and bang on the cell door. Ten of us ended up in front of the judge, but the case for affray was thrown out due to them being unclear on which of us instigated and participated in the whole situation. As the judge spoke, a few of us burst out laughing, to which he gave us a very stern telling off, but the seriousness of the situation did not faze me. I left the lodge worse than when I had arrived, with a worse temper and a permanent scar to prove it.

It had been a long while since I had seen my mum, and after she told me my dad said I could not see my brother and sister, I decided I did not want a relationship with her. She would not even try to understand how devastating this whole situation had been for me. Up until then I had jumped to her defence whenever social services questioned why she never made much of an effort to see me in spite of the evidence they showed me that they provided support for her to do so. It slowly dawned on me that she was far from this helpless person who did not know was going on.

Sometimes my siblings sneaked the odd phone call to me, and when I spoke to them, I felt tremendous guilt for speaking up and leaving. They were placed on a child protection register when I left, but my dad still continued to rule them with fear. For a long time, I felt selfish for leaving. After all, I was their big sister, who was meant to look out for them, but I was not there, and now they were suffering the aftereffects of me speaking out about the abuse. I constantly beat myself up about my decision but on the other hand, knew it was the only way. But I never reckoned on how difficult this path would be and felt I deserved the difficult life I was now leading.

In June 1991 I was placed in a care home outside London, which I thought might be a chance of a fresh start for me, the chance I needed to face the deep-seated problems I had. Chalvington Boarding School was a therapeutic kids' home where young people with emotional problems could get the help needed. I made friends easily, and everybody thought I was cool because of my street style and my dancing, but then again, maybe it had more to do with the fact that out of sixteen young people in the house, I was one of only two black kids there, which may have been fascinating, as Seaford was a middle-class white town in the middle of nowhere.

When I and the other black girl went out into Seaford's version of a high street, we would play "spot the black face." This was a place that did not cater to black people, as the record shop had no ragga, or soul music, and the nearest they had to any of this music was Lisa Stanfield smash-hit single at the time called "Been Around the World." I would go up to London every fortnight to visit Patricia or friends to get up-to-date music tapes and eat Jamaican food. I would also stop at a black hair shop to pick up supplies of pink hair oil and gel for my hair after I had visited the hairdresser to get my hair relaxed and the sides shaved with funky patterns put in. Then I made the hour-and-forty-five-minute train journey back to Seaford. Sometimes my social worker would bring me down what she would call my "ethnic supplies," but that was not often, because she didn't come that often.

I made a very good friend while I was there, called Mason Riley, who was my age, white, and a ragga music lover like myself. He was from North London and knew what was down, as he was street-wise, so we instantly had a lot in common. Although I got on with well with some of the staff and kids, I could not relate to them, as they came from other areas that were more closeted than London. Mason's mum was nice and often invited me down for weekends and would make up the spare room for me. We had a good friendship, which I did my best not to manipulate, as I had done with most of my other friendships I had. My relationships with Patricia and Mason meant a lot to me.

I still had a lot of moments at Chalvington where I would lose my temper and hit staff and other kids, which always resulted in me being restrained until I calmed down. When things were not going my way, I would try to cause trouble amongst some of the other kids. I was always influential in my peer group in whatever children's home I landed in and would use the fact that others found me intimidating to my advantage.

Chalvington was a lot calmer than the Middlesex Lodge, as most girls there were hype on acting out. I had to attend therapy with a psychotherapist once a week, plus attend group and individual sessions with my key worker. I found it hard to focus and, far from trying to deal with the issues that caused my behaviour, tried to avoid the subject. When I was around people, I was always joking about, giggling at any and everything. The other kids liked being around me because I was fun and lively, but the truth was, I hated being me and did not have a good opinion of myself at all. Behind closed doors I spent a lot of time crying, wishing I was dead, and many times I tried half-hearted suicide attempts by taking Paracetamol. I always took enough to cause damage but not quite enough to kill myself; I just wanted the pain inside to go away.

I found a new way to relieve my inner pain between smoking weed when I could get it and alcohol; I started self-harming. I had seen the girls at Middlesex Lodge do it many times, and most of the girls and boys at Chalvington self-harmed too. Even though I was surrounded with others who did it, I never felt tempted to try, but now I was feeling worse than ever and decided I had nothing to lose by trying it. I was allowed to keep my razor, as I was not identified as a harmer before I came to the Chalvington Lodge. I went into the bathroom and locked the door. Sitting on the edge of the bath, I pressed the razor into my arm until I could feel the blade sear through my skin. Moving it away, I could see the pink flesh underneath my broken black skin, which trickled through burgundy red blood slowly. I repeated the process over and over again, saying under my breath that I was no good. After a while the anger and disgust at me subsided, and in its place came a strange sense of peace and calm . My arm was stinging and sore, but it was a bearable pain compared to the pain I felt inside. Looking at the blood reminded me that I was still alive, as I needed to see it to believe it.

Chalvington was the first home since being in care that I felt settled enough to unpack my belongings as, up until this point, I had lived out of my black bags. I had my own room and got to decorate it the way I wanted. Feeling this settled did not happen overnight; it took around three months for me to feel this comfortable. I began to open up to some of the female staff, but I was still very wary of men.

Chalvington closed down nine months later in March 1992, due to lack of funding, and I was very distressed. I was finally opening up and talking and had made some progress in the few months I had been there and could not believe I would have to move again. Social services promised this would be a permanent placement for me.

The head of the home called a meeting to tell us, and most of the staff and kids were crying, asking the staff where we would go. They were given just four weeks to find us all new placements, and my social services had nowhere to put me, so I was sent back to Middlesex Lodge.

After being back at Middlesex Lodge for six weeks, social services found another placement for me, another therapeutic children's home, called Cumberlow Lodge in south London. By the time I reached there in June 1992, I was very wild. During my second stay at the lodge, I began to abscond frequently, and just as I earned my time out by doing all the things I was supposed to without any trouble, I would blow it by staying out into the early hours in the morning. My friend and I would find ourselves down in Harlesden and Neasden, as she had a boyfriend down those ends who knew where to party and get weed. Curfew was nine o'clock, so when we did not turn up, the usual procedure for the lodge was to inform the police and our relevant social services.

At Cumberlow the regime was different, more relaxed. I did not have to earn points or, when I misbehaved, be escorted to the shops, and I was not in the sticks in Seaford anymore, where everything was alien to me culturally. I did not always operate within the boundaries set by adults and always thought I knew best. The worst consequence Cumberlow dished out for bad behaviour was withholding pocket money or grounding me, but I would walk out anyway. I made some internal progress while I was there, as I began to realise I really did not know who Yvonne really was. Any time I began to feel depressed, I would distract myself by doing the usual drinking, smoking, and acting out. If group therapy sessions got hard, I would start arguments. I did enjoy some of the activities there and learned how to play musical instruments like the drums and the piano. English and art classes were my best lessons, and I won a couple of awards for my poetry. There were a couple of staff members I got on well with. Their names were Susan and Kerry; they always gave me cuddles and really cared for me. Sometimes I let my guard down with them and showed a softer side, but as I caught myself doing this too much, I would put my guard back up. I believed if I showed this side, people would hurt me. In my childhood I was naturally an open child, and being trusting and vulnerable had left me confused, angry, and damaged.

I now was now sixteen years old and felt burdened beyond my young years. The different masks I learned to help me cope during and since the sexual abuse had worn me out, but I had no choice but to keep up the pretence. I thought that it was not acceptable to be myself, as I was not good enough, so I became whatever people or the situation called me to be. I was a liar and fantasist who made up stories about me and my upbringing to impress people because the reality was too shameful. I had a couple of boyfriends along the way, but due to my past abuse, I would not have sex with them, which led to them being frustrated with me. They would say if I really loved them I would do it, and I tried my hardest to go further but would freeze up when it got too heated. So I ended up being dumped because they felt I was leading them on. I spent a lot of my time at Cumberlow staying out all night instead of focusing on issues I believed I could run from. I got an A+ in General Certificate of Secondary Education English while I was there—an achievement for me and the only qualification I left the care system with. I did regret not using my time at Cumberlow as well as I could have.

Teenage Mum

I met Jason in 1993 when I was sixteen years old, and I thought he was the most wonderful person in the world. He was charming and good looking, and I never thought he would be interested in a girl like me. I was very naive when I was young, and that, coupled with my low self-esteem, led me to believe that everyone was better than me and that I was unworthy of being loved. We both were dating other people at the time, but it did not matter to me. The guy I was dating was a nice guy, and whatever I wanted he brought me: name-brand trainers, clothes, and jewellery, but the problem was that I was manipulative and incapable of offering him the love he wanted, so I used him.

When I met Jason, I dumped the guy I was dating straightaway, and after a few weeks, Jason dumped his girl. Jason and I spent a lot of time together over those first few weeks, and I was completely smitten. I was insecure and resorted to doing what I usually did: telling lies about myself in order for him to feel that he wanted to be with me. I made out that I came from a big family, that I had lots of jewellery, a car, but the most despicable lie I ever told him was that I had lost my virginity at fourteen years old to a guy I dated in the adventure playground. I desperately wanted to be his girlfriend at the time and ended up doing the one thing I was scared of doing—having sex. Because I had nothing within me that made me feel I was worth so much more, I ended up selling myself short.

I was having dinner at Cumberlow one evening and experienced the most terrible stomach cramps, worse than any period pain I ever experienced in my life. Loretta, my key worker, pulled me aside and asked me when I had last had a period. I told her, but she insisted that I have a pregnancy test. Pregnancy never crossed my mind . In fact, those types of situations are not what you think about at sixteen, and I had never even seen anyone my age pregnant. So imagine my shock when two pregnancy tests came out positive. I fell to the floor screaming and crying. I had only been going out with Jason six weeks. Loretta tried to comfort me, but I was in shock. How could I be a mum when I could not even look after myself? Where would I live? How would I look after it? Questions raced through my head. I could not believe this was happening to me yet again. Lying about myself had gotten me into trouble. I had really messed up big time. Why did I pretend to Jason that I had already had sex? In spite of all the confusing thoughts, a strong protective feeling came over me, and I made a choice that I would not get rid of my baby. It was as simple as that. In the space of a few minutes, I went from crying hysterics calling the baby "it," to calling it "my baby." My mind was made up.

I decided to go and tell Jason at his house, but he was not very welcoming to me. I tried to stress the urgency of why I was there, to no avail, and ended up telling him on his doorstep. He let me in after that. We were both so young and stupid—not just in our actions but also in our thinking, because for us, the future only went as far as tomorrow—not years or decades to come, and that was evident in the way we talked about the baby.

After a few bumpy weeks of arguments, we decided that come what may, we would stick together and try to make a family unit for this baby. To Jason's credit, at the time, he really tried to do the right thing by sticking by me, even when he had to face much disapproval from his family, who thought I was far too young to have a baby. But as my baby grew inside of me, people's comments did not matter. I wanted to do the right thing and take responsibility for the choice

I had made, which was done out of love. It was this strong love that motivated me to stop smoking weed and cigarettes and gave me the strength to cope with the stares and looks of disapproval from total strangers who looked at me like I was a tramp as I walked past them on the street. I looked after my health more and learned how to cook various meals. My behaviour changed dramatically. Although I was argumentative and confrontational at times, I stopped lashing out and getting in violent confrontations because I did not want to harm my baby. For the first time in my life, I started to think about consequences to choices I always made in the heat of the moment, which was a huge personal achievement for me.

In between moments of personal clarity and sugar-coated, happily-ever-after feelings I believed having this baby would bring, I had to deal with the harsh realities of stepping out into the world and providing a good environment for my baby to be brought up in. I had to move from Cumberlow, as it was not a suitable place to bring up a baby. My social worker suggested a foster placement, but I wanted my own flat, which she said was not possible, as they wanted me to be somewhere I could be assessed to see how I managed with the baby. If it went well, then I could go into independent living. Social services were concerned that I would become isolated if I moved into a flat straightaway because of my history with depression. They wanted to make sure there was support in place for my final move out of the care system. I was hesitant at first because of my bad experience with the first foster parent I had when I entered the care system, but it made sense, as I needed a family environment so I could learn how to look after the baby.

A meeting was arranged with Veronica, my new foster parent, and I went to stay a couple of times as part of a trial period. Veronica was caring, kind, and very supportive during my pregnancy. I was not sad to leave Cumberlow, as I was fed up of being in mainstream care and wanted my own space. Living at Veronica's allowed me to have that to an extent, as I lived in her second house with her cousin.

Veronica owned two houses next door to each other. The first house was her main house, and my four younger foster sisters lived in that house with her. While I lived under her care, I was not treated as an outsider and was free to come and go between the two houses.

Jason continued to be supportive and came over occasionally but was not allowed to stay overnight. I was around four months pregnant when I began to sense that something was not right with Jason, and on one occasion when I had stayed over at his house while he was at work, I searched through his chest of drawers and found a letter from his other girlfriend, who was on holiday in Jamaica. I was devastated to find out he was betraying me and went straight back and told my foster mum. She told me to photocopy the letter, as she said if I confronted him with it he would try to rip it up. I did confront him, and that was exactly what he did. He cried and said it was a mistake. I believed him so I forgave him. What was I to do? I was sixteen and pregnant; I did not want to bring up this baby on my own. Unfortunately I was to find out this was a sign as to what life with Jason would be like.

Social services got in contact with my natural mum and told her I was pregnant. I had not seen or had any contact with her since I was fourteen years old, but I decided I would try to give her another chance. She was every bit the doting grandmother, buying baby clothes and equipment for the baby. There were still issues between us, which she still would not discuss. I naively thought that after not seeing me all this time, she would have had time to reflect upon what had happened and want to talk. This was not the case, as all she wanted to talk about was shopping, what bargains she found, and what buy one, get one free offers were on down at Tesco's. It was just like being at home again. I needed her, but, as usual, she was incapable of offering any emotional support because she was emotionally inaccessible. I know she believed that if she bought me things it would make up for what happened when I was a child. But her material gifts were not important to me, as all I wanted from her was love, support, and acceptance. Deep down I knew I was not going to get this from her because how could she give me something that she did not have?

I continued to let her buy me because I wanted her in my life, and for now, it was on her terms. I did not have the energy to broach the subject with her, as I had to focus on trying to be positive for my baby.

My belly got bigger and bigger, and my clothes became tighter and tighter. I was seven months pregnant and still trying to squeeze into size-eight leggings. Social services had all but dumped me at Veronica's, and she had to fight tooth and nail to get them to cough up extra money for maternity clothes and baby items. They did not seem to care what happened to me, so everything with them became a fight for my rights.

I was in labour thirteen hours, and if it had not been for Jason supporting me, it would have been more difficult. The nurses were very rude to me and offered no support or advice; I was just left to get on with it.

During my pregnancy I was not offered the chance to go to birth classes, so I did not know what to expect. Every so often the nurses would come and check to see how far I was dilated and check the gas and air supply then disappear. To say I was terrified would be an understatement. I had no idea what I should be doing, and the labour seemed to go on forever and ever. I was exhausted and scared, but Jason was supportive, encouraging me to keep going, and in the end, I got there. I gave birth on the third of January at 5:40 a.m. to a beautiful little girl I named Sophia, who was very tiny—weighing only four pounds three ounces, not much more than a bag and half of sugar. She was not a premature baby, as she was born at thirty-eight weeks, but she had problems feeding and was a little starved of oxygen during the birth, so she had to go into the special care baby unit straight after the birth. I had to go straight into emergency surgery, as I had lost a lot of blood due to after-pregnancy complications. It was a stressful time, but as soon as I was allowed to see my baby, all the pain just melted away. I could not believe I could produce something so beautiful, and when I held her tiny body in the crook of my arm, I knew I had made the right decision.

Sophia was only in the baby care unit three days and had made great progress, so the doctor said I was allowed to take her home. Jason had been with me all this time and helped in whatever way he could, but we had not even left the hospital when we started arguing. Since the birth I felt like I was floating on a cloud with my baby and Jason. I had my own little family and felt very grown up. There were major problems between Jason and me, but I thought it would all work out because we were a family now and because I loved him and wanted to be the best mother I could for Sophia as well.

To everyone's surprise, I adapted to motherhood well. Veronica showed me how to bathe and look after her properly and how to get into a routine so that I could take care of myself. There were times when I thought I could not cope, especially when Sophia would not stop crying. I thought I would crack. My depression had crept back, but I held it together for most of the time. Being a mum was tiring and emotionally challenging; I never had enough time to myself. Veronica looked after Sophia a few hours some days, but there were times I wished I could go to parties with my friends. Most days I took Sophia to Jason's house. He was a loving and caring father. He did help with all of the duties with the baby at his house but did not do nights, as I was living at Veronica's and he was not allowed to sleep over. Tension built in our relationship real quick, as Jason complained I spent too much time with Sophia and not enough time with him. I felt bad, but my main priority was Sophia. We chose to have her, and I thought he was being unfair. Sophia was a baby and had no one else but us to rely on. I could hardly just leave her on her own.

Sophia was three months old when I was given my first flat. I was seventeen years old but felt mature. I was so excited about living on my own, as it meant Jason could stay over and the start of us becoming a real family. There was not much money to buy anything for the flat, as help from social services was nonexistent. Veronica continued to give me all the support I needed and helped me get a grant for five hundred pounds from the department of social security. It may seem like a lot of money, but by the time I bought a few basics like a bed and fridge, the money was gone.

The pressure of my new responsibilities became too much for me to bear, and soon enough I started smoking weed and cigarettes again. Every week when I cashed my income support at the post office, at least ten to twenty pounds of it would go to smoking. Besides smoking weed, Jason was also selling it, as he was not working. My old insecurities reared their ugly head again, and my relationship with Jason was not helping. We had grown apart, and the constant arguing was wearing me down. I found out he was seeing yet another girl toward the end of our relationship. This really hurt me, as I had given my all to him. I desperately wanted Sophia to grow up in a two-parent family and was holding on with everything I had in myself, which was not much. I decided to go down to the flat he was staying in with his friend to talk to him, as he did not stay much round my flat anymore. I knocked on the door with Sophia in the buggy, and when he opened the door, he tried to push me away, swearing at me, while he had another girl in the flat. I left in the end, as Jason was becoming more and more aggressive. Communication between us went downhill very quickly, and by the time Sophia was six months old, our relationship was over.

Psychologists talk about the importance of how a good upbringing shapes a child as they grow up, especially in the choices they make in the relationships they end up in and how they interact with others. My own dad was abusive, and I witnessed the way he treated my mum, and I clearly saw how I ended up in the relationship I was in. When I was sexually abused by my dad, I believed if I did everything he asked and was a good girl, my actions would be the deciding factor on making him stop, as I felt I must have done something wrong for him to do what he did to me. I thought the same way in my relationship with Jason. If I tried being the girl he wanted me to be, this would make him happy, and in return, he would give me the love and affirmation I had desperately craved my whole life.

I have come to learn now that if you do not have that strong foundation in yourself from a loving and stable childhood and other positive factors, you never will find it outside yourself, especially in someone else. Jason and I were a recipe for disaster because both of us did not have strong upbringings and were insecure, with bad tempers to boot. We were young and had no real solid example of how a relationship between a man and a woman should be, let alone a parenting one. I felt I had morphed into a modern-age version of my mum, who I watched give away her whole soul just to please a man.

It was a lonely and unhappy road that I choose to walk down, as all I let Jason do was destroy me. Every negative comment he made chipped away at my self-esteem, and soon enough I went from being his girlfriend to his other woman. He would tell me I was not good enough for him and that he did not want me but constantly kept coming back. He told me I was nothing, and I believed him, for what did I have to show for my life? I loved Sophia with all my heart, but I had no job, did not love myself, and was suffering from depression. The only glimmer of light that gave me some hope was my belief that I could have a proper family with Jason. In him I attached all my dreams of love and having a proper family before it was taken from me at nine years old. I overrode the fact that there were serious psychological issues that existed that were damaging in my family but could not get past this ideal family illusion in my head. I thought in order to get my dream, I should put up with Jason's behaviour towards me for the sake of Sophia. So even though we were not a couple anymore, I would still cook his dinner, plait his hair, sleep with him, and let him stay the night—basically use me how he wanted. Then, the morning after, I cooked his breakfast; he would make his plans and then leave. It was the same if he and his girlfriend would have an argument. He would come round, and I would let him use me as his safety net because I wanted his attention, and when everything was all right, he would be off again. Sometimes his girlfriend would ring while we were in the same room. I knew it was a girlfriend because his demeanour would change and he would go into another room. It was an eye opener, as I got to see from another side how he must have acted when I was his girlfriend and he was at his other girlfriend's house. When he would come back in the room, I would act as if it did not bother me, but inside, my heart would break.

One summer when Sophia was around fifteen months old, a friend of mine invited me to the afro hair and beauty show. It was an event that took place every year, and there would be hair exhibitions and stalls where you could buy products. It was a good atmosphere, and I really enjoyed myself. I did not have money to buy new clothes, so I ended up mixing and matching whatever I had in my wardrobe, and a friend of mine was a hairdresser, so she did my hair. It was one of a handful of times I had been out since having Sophia, and I was nervous, as I had not been around lots of people in a long time. But when we got there, I soon got over my shyness and ended up having a good time. It was just what I needed, and it boosted my confidence. A couple of people even commented on my hairstyle. I missed Sophia but was not worried, as her dad was at my house looking after her.

His friends were just leaving when I arrived home, but as soon as Jason saw me, his mood immediately changed from laughing with his friends to being aggressive. He and his friends had been smoking weed, as my flat smelt strongly of it and his eyes were red. He said something rude to me, and I made the mistake of answering him back. There was a look in his eyes I had not seen before, even when we had had heated arguments that made me feel scared. He was more intimidating than usual, and I sensed danger. I started shaking, but I managed to pick up Sophia and started to walk toward the front door. Jason then punched me straight in the mouth while Sophia was in my arms, splitting my lip and chipping my tooth. My mouth was full of blood, and my top was covered as well. I only just managed to get Sophia into her buggy, which was outside the bathroom near the front door, when all of a sudden, Jason grabbed me by the neck and slammed me into the bathroom wall above the sink. I could not breathe and was struggling for air, but all I could think about was Sophia, who was screaming the house down, crying for her mother. It didn't faze him one bit; he was like a maniac, frothing at the mouth with the veins by his eyes bulging out, screaming at me that I better watch myself. I was crying, and Sophia was crying too as I tried to manoeuvre the buggy down the flight of stairs while dabbing a tissue on my cut lip. Jason stood at the front door screaming obscenities at me. The fact Sophia was crying did not even stop him. I walked to the end of my road, and for about ten minutes, I stood there, not knowing where to go. Sophia was still crying, and I tried my best to soothe her, but as I had left so hastily, I forgot her baby bag. The only person I knew who would help me was my foster mum, Veronica, so I walked the twenty minutes it took to get there, as I did not have any money.

Veronica saw my mouth, and I told her what happened. She was livid, to say the least. Veronica, her friend, and I went back round my flat so I could get Sophia's stuff. I fully expected Jason not be there, so I was surprised when I found him there with his friend. While I was gone in the space of a couple of hours, Jason had smashed up everything in my flat. I only had a few belongings, but he overturned chairs, smashed up my wardrobe, mirror, and table. He even went as far as opening up creams and powders and pouring them onto the carpets. Veronica was mad, and she stood right in his face, asking him why he hit me. He replied that it was because I was talking back to him. Veronica really let him have it, and he did not talk back to her. I was really low about being hit by him, but I rationalized to myself that I deserved it. I am not any angel and was argumentative and difficult at the best of times. Maybe if I had not talked back to him, he would not have reacted like that.

I was angry for a few days, but in the end, I let him back in my life because I loved him. When we met up to talk, he seemed remorseful, crying and apologetic about his behaviour. I was naïve and believed it was a one off incident that would not happen again. Veronica, my mum, and other people I had in my life at the time thought I was crazy for letting him back in, but their protestations about him made me more defiant. The fact that nobody in my life liked him did not bother me. To people who did not know what he could be like, they were completely taken in by him. His family were well aware of his behaviour but treated him as some type of loveable rogue. He was a charmer, and he used that skill well to win people over. I thought I would never get another man as charming as him, so I put up with his aggressive and negative behaviour toward me.

It was only a few months later that he punched me in the stomach and winded me so bad that I fell to my knees on the floor. I could not even cry, as I was in so much pain, and I will never forget the words he said as he stood over me as I cowered on the floor—that no wonder my dad abused me and that I was pathetic and weak. On numerous occasions he threatened to kill me and called me derogatory names, but no matter how much his words hurt me, I still clung on to him for dear life. I had no self-respect and began self-harming again, as it was the only way I could get the pain out from inside. Trying to love him was like walking on broken glass. Even though I knew the outcome would cause me great pain, I continued to go back. There were a couple of times his family was in the vicinity of me being attacked by him. One time I was in his bedroom. We had an argument. I went to go out the door, and he pinned me up against the wall with a switchblade pressed into my neck, threatening to kill me. His mum must have heard a commotion and knocked the door, asking me a couple of times if I was all right. I said yes, of course, as I did not want to make the situation worse. Another time he tried to hit me, and I ran out of the house, only to be greeted by some of his relatives returning. I begged one of them to let me get in her car, as I was scared. She said no at first, but then, with great reluctance, she let me sit in the car. If it was not for one of his aunts physically sitting on him, he probably would have beaten me there and then.

I did not really tell anyone at the time the extent of what I was really going through because I was scared of what they would say, especially because of what happened the first time. My mum and Veronica kind of knew and advised me to dump him, but for me it was not as easy, because in my warped mind, I thought it was love. He knew I would take him back no matter what he did, as he knew I was happy to accept any little crumbs of hope he had to offer. A crumb of a compliment he sometimes gave, a crumb of a chance of us getting back together was what kept me holding on.

I spent a lot of time in tears smoking weed, drinking alcohol, and listening to sad K-Ci and JoJo love songs when I put Sophia to bed. Their music at the time spoke to me about love overcoming the odds in a toxic relationship that would not work out, no matter how I tried. For 80 percent of the time, he treated me badly, but it was the 20 percent that kept me hanging on. It was the 20 percent that blindsided me and kept me in denial about my situation, as well as the determination for Sophia not to grow up in a single-parent household. I did not want to be a failure at the only positive in my life. Like a broken rag doll that had been used for years, ripped and falling apart, I hung on. Jason could be the sweetest person in the world one minute and abusive and mean the next—like Jekyll and Hyde.

I was nineteen when I found out I was eight weeks pregnant by Jason again. I went to the doctor for a routine medical, and she did a test. I wanted to keep it, but when I discussed it with Jason, we both agreed it would not be possible. I was struggling to make ends meet and could just cope, even though I now had a part-time job, so I ended up having a termination. I was about eleven weeks when it was done. I spent a lot of time trying to put it off because I did not want to go through with it. I was disgusted with myself and felt ashamed. My friend came with me to the clinic in 1996, which was hidden away behind tall trees and bushes in South London. Even as you walked up to the building, it looked like a very dark and frightening place. I had to sign a consent form, and that was it—no counselling sessions or anyone to talk to about my decision. The nurse gave me a scan, and I could clearly see the life growing inside me. Another nurse came in and reprimanded the scan nurse because she did not put the screen up so that I could not see, but it was too late. I had already seen the baby on the screen. I turned my head to the other side and cried.

I came round from the aesthetic in a lot of pain. My friend was sitting by my bed, and she started talking to me. A nurse brought me tea and a Twix, but I just felt completely sick and empty. All around me women were crying. It was a horrible, sterile place that lacked love. I had to wait a couple of hours before I could go home, and then when the time came, the clinic packed me off with some antibiotics, painkillers, and leaflets on how to look after myself over the next few weeks. I had to take a cab back home, as I was feeling weak. Jason was sad about it, and we tried to be supportive to each other for a while, but the situation between us resumed back to what it had always been, as we were not in a relationship. It was a weird feeling over the few weeks afterwards, as my body still thought it was carrying a baby, so I still had a pregnant stomach. I cried every time I looked at myself.

Having a termination affected me deeply, and every time I looked at Sophia, I felt guilty and ashamed. I coped with Sophia as a baby; why did I think I could not cope with two? Money was an issue the first time round, but it did not stop me having her. I struggled with my conscience for many years and until this day cannot read or look at issues to do with abortion.

Depression and Finding God

My depression had become really bad, and I did want to deal with my life anymore. My mind continually ran on suicidal thoughts, and I believed I would be better off dead. I could barely function at the best of times but dealt with it the way I had always done—act outgoing and pretend I was happy in front of people, then, as soon as I was behind closed doors, smoke weed and drink alcohol and cry.

I had a part-time job at Littlewoods as a cashier working sixteen hours a week and liked working there, as it gave me a chance to build my confidence and help take my mind off my problems. On the days when I was not working, I would drop Sophia to nursery and go straight back home to smoke weed and stay under the duvet the whole day until it was time to pick her up. My bed was my safe haven and comforting, a place where I could stop the pretence. Weed became my best friend, and what was so sad about my addiction to it was there would be times I would be short of money for bills because I had spent it on weed. Earlier on, when I first started to smoke, I was able to use common sense and limit myself to a ten-pound bag a week, and when it ran out, I would stick to cigarettes and alcohol. I was always borrowing money off people and found it hard to pay them back. Sometimes, Sophia's main diet staples were

Weetabix and boiled potatoes mashed up with tinned spaghetti or beans on top, as money was tight. I was disgusted at my behaviour but felt powerless to change as I slipped further into despair. It became a vicious cycle of destructiveness, repulsion, and beating myself up about my behaviour, which ended back at depression. In spite of how irresponsible I was at times with money, I made sure Sophia never wanted for clothes, and my mum and Jason helped out whenever they could. I always made sure she looked presentable. Everyone always commented that Sophia always looked nice.

It was almost as if my life began to crash in after having Sophia. Not that it was her fault in any way; I think, in having her, it forced a lot of unresolved feelings that I spent a lot of time avoiding to a head. Letting Jason use me, the abuse I suffered as a child plaguing me in the form of nightmares, and trying to deal with several other personal issues at the same time left me emotionally worn out and anxious about even the smallest things that came up in life.

My brother and sister were getting kicked out of my mum and dad's house every other week because Dad kept telling Mum to pick between them and him, but then he would change his mind and let them back in. In the end, Dad took my brother's stuff, including his mattress, and threw them out of his bedroom window in front of his friends on our estate, and a few weeks later, he kicked my sister out because he said she reminded him of me. Mum made them leave for good, so the responsibility fell on to me to look out for them. My brother stayed with me for a while, as he had people after him and needed to get out of Battersea, and then my sister stayed with me on and off for a couple of years. I was very angry at my mum and could not believe she could be so cold to her own children. Her behaviour showed she did not of love any of us, because she continued to make selfish decisions based around her needs.

When they stayed, especially my sister, they helped me with Sophia. I found it hard to live with them at times, but could not turn my back on them because I loved them and felt it was my fault that they were in this position. So whenever they needed me, I tried to be there.

My sister pretended it did not bother her, but I could tell she was hurt, as she believed she had a good relationship with Mum. When Mum made the choice that my sister had to go, she slept on a landing in one of the tower blocks on the estate for a few nights. My nan would not let her stay round her house because she did not want to upset my dad. I tried to fill the void that Mum left by supporting them emotionally and practically. I was being stretched in every direction because I tried my best to be all things to everyone.

My sister was going out with a very nice guy called Gareth who had an older brother named Ryan. My sister and Gareth thought it would be a good idea to play matchmaker and set us up on a date in the summer of 1997. Jason had been trying to remain faithful to his girlfriend, so I was rendered useless, and to be honest, I was relieved. I was now twenty years old and had been on this destructive merry-go-round with Jason for four years, and I wanted to get off. I was excited about meeting Ryan, as my sister kept telling me how nice he was; she was more excited than me. We knocked on the front door, and I kept asking my sister if I looked all right. She reassured me that I looked nice. Gareth opened the door, and my sister introduced us. Then I was introduced to Ryan. We both said hello and made small talk. The first thought that came to my head about Ryan was that he was just my type—dark skinned and good looking with nice eyes. He was very gentlemanly, which was unusual for guys my age, and kept asking if I wanted anything. In no time, we were chatting away like we had known each other our whole lives, and I felt extremely comfortable with him. By the end of the day, we decided to have a relationship.

Ryan was a good man, and I was happy with him. He was the first person I felt comfortable being myself around. Whether I was having a bad day or feeling down, he would just hold me and tell me he loved me. He never called me names or put me down, and we had a lot of fun together, going out to dinner or a wine bar. I introduced him to Sophia, and she loved playing with him, as every time he came round, she would get her ball and badger him to play football. It was a nice period in my life, and I enjoyed our relationship immensely. We talked about our insecurities, dreams, and aspirations, and we also had debates about subjects like Christianity, which got quite passionate, as I believed Jesus died for my sins and was the way to eternal life, and Ryan at the time believed if you were a good person, that was enough for you to get into heaven.

I would make Ryan dinner, and we would do little things that meant a lot for each other. When Ryan came round, he always brought me roses and a box of Ferrero Rocher chocolates, and the same would be waiting for me when I would go round his house. I genuinely felt loved by him, so I don't know why after a nearly a year together, I ended up cheating with Jason. It happened only the once, but immediately I felt damned and decided to tell Ryan straightaway. My sister and friends said I should not tell him, but I knew it was the right thing to do. Ryan did not deserve to be treated like that. He took the news surprisingly well, and his reaction was not what I expected at all. Obviously, he was hurt and upset, but he did not shout or scream at me. But what surprised me the most was that Ryan was willing to forgive me and wanted us to stay together. I could not forgive myself for what I had done and felt he deserved someone better than me, so I called it a day.

Being with Ryan taught me so much in regards to how I wanted to be treated and the potential I had as a woman to give. Still, I could not make the connection in my mind that the treatment I received was how it naturally was supposed to be. Jason still had his woman and never had any intention, as always, of leaving her. Jason just did not like the fact I had a boyfriend, and when I ended it with Ryan, he still continued living his life. The good experience I had with Ryan made me want more than what I was getting out of life, but because I was constantly negative about myself, I dared not believe that I could achieve much.

I started to question my existence and wanted answers about why I was having a hard time in my life. Jason's mum was a nice woman, and she had become a born-again Christian when Sophia was six months old. It happened during the time when we were looking for a church for Sophia's dedication. It was also during this time that I became more aware of God, as I heard many wonderful things through church sermons about his power and love. Over the years that followed, Jason's mum and I began to have a good relationship even though her son and I were not together. We had many discussions on Christianity, and I used to ask her questions about God and Jesus. No matter what negative things I would say about myself, she would always tell me that Jesus came for someone like me and that he loved me just the way I was; all I needed to do was sincerely ask Jesus into my life. I believed Jesus died for me but did not understand how he could love someone like me, who had felt unlovable her entire life.

Sophia was growing up to be a beautiful loving girl. She was only five years old, but she was polite and kind and always told me she loved me. I know it was not easy for her growing up with a mother who had problems with depression, as, at times, I found it hard to interact with her, and having to hear and witness the dysfunctional behaviour from Jason and me did not help her either. I tried to be the best mum I could but felt I fell short a lot of the time because of my struggle with depression. If there was one thing I was good at, it was being loving, and I made sure Sophia knew she was loved because I would tell her so many times every day and I was forever kissing and cuddling her. All the care and attention I did not receive in my childhood, I gave to her. I did not want her growing up feeling unloved and like a spare part. Her happiness was important to me. I was not shown how to be a good mum emotionally and could not use my own mum as a reference point, but the way I felt about her in my heart brought a lot of goodness out of me, and naturally I knew what I needed to do.

My mum continued to visit every other weekend, laden with bags of food shopping. I had had enough of our relationship, and the core problem was the constant pushing under the carpet of the incidents that happened in my childhood. No matter how I attempted to broach the subject, the response was always the same: if your dad did these things to you, then why haven't you confronted him? Her response was the emotional carrot she used to dangle in front of my nose, so one Sunday I dropped Sophia down to my foster mum's house and took a train down to Clapham Junction. I had not been back to the house since the day I had been taken by social services eight years earlier. I was not scared to go back there and, as a matter of fact, felt defiant. I prayed to God to protect and help me and felt a sense of calm.

I knocked on the door, and my mum opened it. She was shocked to see me standing there, and the look on her face was one of horror. She told me to go away, but I was not having any of it and pressed past her and walked into the front room. My brother was there, as he was visiting Mum, and when my dad came down the stairs, my brother stood between us. Dad started swearing and shouting, but I remained calm and looking him straight in the eyes, I said, "Now that we are all here, tell the truth. Were you not sexually abusing me for five years?"

Dad would not answer the question and continued to talk over me, threatening to throw me out of the house. Mum asked me to leave, so I asked her if now she believed me; she said nothing. I rephrased my question and asked him if he was not sexually interfering with me for five years. He responded by calling me a liar and telling me that even the police did not believe me, but I knew this was a lie and told him so. I told him that he could lie in front of Mum, but God and I knew the truth about what he did and that was all that mattered. He had lost his temper by now and threatened to hit me. Up to this point, I had been calm, but I lost my temper and went mad. I said to him I was not the little girl he used to terrorize anymore and if he put his hand on me, it would be the last thing he would do in this house. I was so angry that he felt he could talk to me in that way, and I was almost willing him to do it so I could vent years of frustration down on him. My brother was behind me holding my arms, and Dad was apparently being held back by my mum. I don't believe he would have hit me, because if that was the case, he could easily have gotten past my mum to do it. My brother and mum were begging me to leave, so in the end, I did, making as much noise as possible. I stood outside the house on the balcony, shouting out that he was a paedophile and that he would not get away with it.

A couple of weeks later, I met up with my mum outside Arding & Hobbs in Clapham Junction, and bizarrely, she acted as though the visit to the house had not happened. I was a little nervous but decided I needed to know, now I had done what she had asked, if she believed me. Her response was one of disregard for my feelings, and she told me that I needed to forget about what had happened in my past. Tears welled up in my eyes, and I realised that to her, confronting my dad was not about bringing out what happened in the open, but buying her more time in our relationship. She never dreamed I would have the guts to go down the house, and now that I had, it forced her into a corner. There was nothing left to say, so I walked away. I did not want a relationship with her anymore, so I cut all contact with her.

Life still had to go on, and I did not for one minute regret confronting her and my dad, but the despair and feelings of rejection were overwhelming, and the suicidal thoughts continued to present themselves as an easy option, a way out of the pain. Thoughts of Sophia helped me to hold on, but I believed she would be better off without me.

My behaviour reinforced what I believed about myself, and I went through a stage where I became promiscuous. I never had any one-night stands but had a succession of short-term relationships because I was lonely and I thought it would help me get over Jason and build my self-esteem. I reasoned to myself that it was an ideal solution, as I could not give myself emotionally to any man and did not think it would cause me any more harm. I partied often with friends, and my behaviour was not out of place with theirs, as everyone my age I knew behaved the same, as it was part of the whole raving scene of my generation. My mental health deteriorated quickly because I was putting myself in situations that were not helping me build good self-esteem. I hated what I was doing to myself but had no one to blame for my actions but myself. I remember being so disgusted with the way I was treating my body that I scrubbed myself until I bled. At nights I would rock back and forth in my bed, repeating over and over again that I was no good and that there was no room in heaven for fornicators and that I was going to hell.

I screamed out in my bed to God to help me and challenged him, saying, "If you are real, help me turn my life around and save me." I kept repeating it over and over again; then a sense of peace came over me unlike anything I had felt before, like a weight had been lifted off me. I was okay for a couple of days; then I became depressed again, cutting myself more regularly than usual.

Donald and Pat Green were Jason's aunt and uncle whom I had met when Sophia was a baby. I got on well with them, and as they had a daughter who was around the same age as Sophia, I would let her go round to play. They were kind to me, and although they knew some of my problems, I kept them at a distance, like I had always done with everybody else.

Immediately following my disclosure to Pat about wanting to harm myself, she called the pastor of her church who, within a space of a few minutes, came around to my house. Pastor Richard came with a woman from the church whose son had been admitted to the hospital due to having attempted suicide, and she had come to talk me about it. She told me the Lord God understood my pain and that if I allowed him to help, he would. I really wanted help, as I had tried everything up until this point: drugs, alcohol, sex, self-harming, and trying to be what I thought others wanted me to be, and none of it worked. The pastor asked me if I wanted a change in my life, and I said yes. I did not know what I needed to say to receive Jesus into my life, so the pastor gave me the prayer of salvation to repeat after him; Jesus, I am sorry for the things I have done wrong in my life. I ask your forgiveness. Thank you for dying on the cross for me to set me free from my sins. Please come into my life and fill me with your holy spirit and be with me forever. Thank you, Lord Jesus. Amen. That evening I became a born-again Christian, and the decision I made that night marked the beginning of a testing but remarkable new era.

I knew a change had taken place within me, and in the immediate days after I became a born-again Christian, I was so happy that on picking up Sophia one evening from the Greens, I was skipping down the road! It was strange; nothing had changed in my life, and I had the same insecurities and problems I had always had, but I felt peaceful and not as burdened as I usually felt.

From the day I got saved, I did not desire weed again but struggled with smoking cigarettes. I remember a few days later feeling stressed and buying weed to smoke, but when I took a pull from the joint, I immediately felt sick and never touched it again after that. I cannot explain how after smoking weed for eight years the addiction was broken. It was a powerful crutch that I used to deal with my emotions, and although weed is not a physically addictive drug, mentally it was. All I know is the day I let God into my life its hold over me was broken. Instead of coming home and sleeping most of the day away, I started looking for another job and started attending church and reading the Bible. I was making steady progress and told my friends and brother that I had become a Christian, but they just laughed at me. This was enough to put me off attending church as regularly as I did, because I did not like being seen as uncool, and it did not help that I knew no one my age and from the same cultural background that was a Christian. I was still caught up in people pleasing, because if I was not, I would have been able to shrug off the comments and focus on the positives knowing God was bringing into my life. Instead, I backslid away from my faith.

On my twenty-second birthday in August 1999, a card came through the post that was sent by a male who was saying the most derogatory things about me, which sent me into a black hole of depression. I could not understand why anyone would want to send me a card like that. It was so malicious; the words dripped of hate. The words plagued me day and night, and I racked my brain wondering who hated me that much. I showed Jason's Aunt Pat, and she prayed with me about it, but I became paranoid and closed ranks completely, retreating back into my flat.

Bad things come in threes—that's how the saying goes—and the next day when I was at work, my sister came to see me. She was very upset and told me that she had found suggestive pictures of Mum, Dad, and Nan. This revelation sent me into a meltdown and confirmed the fears I had all along that Mum knew what my dad was doing to me. It made me feel like I was part of some sick child-abuse ring. Pat took me to the doctor, and by that very evening, I was admitted into a mental hospital.

The Charter Clinic in Chelsea, South London, is a place where people experiencing psychological, emotional, and mental disorders were referred to after an assessment from a doctor, and I was admitted there, as I was showing symptoms of all three. I had completely broken down and believed my existence was cursed because I was a bad person. It was the only reason that made any sense. Why else would I be experiencing such unfortunate circumstances in my life? It consumed all my thoughts, and no matter how anyone tried to reassure me that this was not the case, it made no difference because I could not think rationally. The doctors placed me on three types of medication—Fluoxetine, Olanzapine, and Zopiclone—which turned me into a living zombie, as the side effects were bad. I would get shakes and trembles without prior warning, sweat profusely, and would feel tired and weak most of the time. The clinic was quite a sterile place, but they tried to make it feel homier by having nice pictures of flowers and other serene imagery on the walls. My room faced out onto the Kings Road, which was a nice road with lots of exclusive shops. I would just stand and stare out the window, which had white metal bars obscuring the view, and watch the world go by. I could not register much and was agitated by small things, such as the noise of cars going by and people talking a lot. I wondered how my life had come to this, and staring through those white bars, I thought my life was over.

Jason's uncle and aunt were a huge support to me at this time. They came to see me with Pastor Richard most days, and they looked after Sophia while I was in the hospital. Jason also came to see me a couple of times too and was upset and asked if my dad and he had done this to me. I could not take in and answer his question because my mind was so fragmented. Each day I took my medication, and the nurses would get me out of bed to go to the counselling groups and relaxation classes. Some days were harder than others, and as much as I wanted to give up, I tried to go, because what I really wanted was for my life to be better. I found it difficult to convey how I was feeling in the counselling group but did enjoy the relaxation classes, as they consisted of lying on a mat on the floor listening to peaceful sounds like waterfalls. Lying still at first was a huge task for me because I was always agitated and anxious. I found it hard to keep still, but soon it became better. In the evening Donald and Pat also brought Sophia down to see me, and seeing her little by little gave me motivation and strength to continue to try to get better. I made some mental progress, and after a month, I was discharged from the clinic, although I still had a long way to go.

I stayed with Jason's uncle and aunt when I came out of the clinic, and they helped me to get back into a routine. I had to give up work, as being on medication made doing daily tasks difficult, but I was glad for the help. I only ever believed they had my best interests at heart, and although they did not have much of a relationship with their nephew, they showed me love. My relationship with them grew during this time, and their children even called me "Auntie" as we grew close, and I gave their daughters my old fashionable clothes, which they always loved. I changed Sophia to the same primary school as their youngest daughter, Ingrid, so that I could continue to get the support I needed and Sophia could spend a lot of time with her cousin. After three months of staying with them, I went back to my own home, and my sister came to stay with me and Sophia. The Greens continued to help pick up Sophia from school, and I also picked up their youngest daughter and had her sleep over some weekends. I appreciated what they had done for me and Sophia and showed my appreciation by doing whatever I could for them, whether it was plaiting Pat's hair or buying gifts for them. I believed our relationship was built on love, trust, and support, at least that was what I thought at the time.

The council moved me a month later to a maisonette in Croydon, and I was happy to leave my flat behind, as it held too many bad memories since leaving care some years before. I started attending psychotherapy since leaving the clinic a few months earlier and found it insightful. This was my fifth attempt at trying therapy, and I knew that in order for me to make a personal improvement, I had to open up and commit myself to the work involved. It sounded easy enough, but making the choice to open up and be honest with myself and fear of rejection and failure kept me an emotional prisoner for so long that the barrier was ingrained in me. Clara Metaxos was my therapist, and I took to her instantly. She was from Greece and had a no-nonsense, caring way of talking about issues. I would see her once a week, and those hourly sessions were my lifeline. She was the only person who could help me try to understand the craziness I was feeling inside due to the trauma I had been through. Psychotherapy helped me to look at the source of my problems that were affecting me and helped me to look on solutions that would make me emotionally healthy, like putting a jigsaw puzzle together, taking each piece, looking on it, and putting it in the right place. Since being abused as child, I just existed and did not know who the real Yvonne was. There were so many questions I wanted answers to and wanted to understand why I was sexually abused, because it had poisoned everything in my life and affected the choices I made. I wanted to learn how to love and accept myself and be able to look in the mirror and be happy with how God made me, not continually look in the mirror and hate what I would see. I wanted to feel safe and secure, as I had grown accustomed to fear and danger, which was not healthy for me emotionally. But most of all, I wanted to able to put the blame for the abuse where it belonged, as I had blamed myself all these years for what my dad had done to me. It was not my fault, but I needed to stop feeding into the lie that because I seemed more outgoing as a child than my sister and brother that it was the reason he chose to abuse me. Instead, I just needed to accept that my dad was responsible for taking my innocence and using it for evil. The blame lay firmly with him, as he took it upon himself to cross the boundaries in our relationship. I struggled with the injustice of the situation because he stole my childhood away from me. The fact that he called me an evil liar made my anger and rage burn even more, and I could not forgive him for what he had done, which ended up poisoning me with hate.

In other sessions we talked about Jason and why I kept trying to justify my attachment to him. Clara told me, in no uncertain terms, that this destructive relationship was feeding into my feelings of low self-esteem and that he was just using me as a crutch. Far from me being weak, as he had told me, Clara said he was in fact the weak one because of his indecision and behaviour. I spent two years with Clara working through these issues, and by the end of our time together, I felt I had a few core pieces of the puzzle in place. I learned that I needed to love myself, to be patient, and not be too hard on myself. Most important of all, I realised I could not be responsible for others behaviour but am only responsible for my choices and how I make their behaviour affect me. Psychotherapy does not magically resolve your issues; it only gives you the tools to work on yourself and enable you to make better choices and decisions. I sensed I was going in the right direction and began to realise that I had a lot to give. I still made many mistakes, especially when it came to letting Jason back in my life, as all it did was reinforce negative thoughts within me. No matter how much I wanted to give up, God would not let me, as he was working everything out for his glory and my good. I soon became strong enough not to rely on as much medication, so the doctor lowered the dosage. Now all I needed to do was put what I learned into place.

I had a relapse a few months later, and I can only take the responsibility for it. I kept up what I learned in therapy for a while, but my problem was that I not setting boundaries with people in my life, and it resulted in me feeling depressed again. I remember feeling so defeated and thought I would never overcome the many problems I had and have the strength to break away from bad influences in my life. Every day I would ask God how many more days I had to live because I wanted to die and did not have the guts to commit suicide. At the top of my road was a funeral home, and each day I passed the shop, I would stand looking through the window at headstones, planning which one I would have for my funeral; it was a really bleak time.

Sophia was coming up to the age I had been when I was sexually abused, and I found it difficult to interact with her at times, as I could see what I must have been like at her age. I believed I let her down, as I had not provided a stable home environment for her. Sophia deserved to have a mother who was emotionally well, who could give her the quality time and love that she deserved and needed not the uncertainty that my problems were causing. I did not want her growing up with the same insecurities I had and struggle in her relationship with me like I did with my mum, because I loved her so much. Financially I was a mess and owed around seven thousand pounds to different companies. I was still on medication and still found it hard to cope with a daily routine, so Croydon social services appointed a social worker to visit me fortnightly to offer support and help. My social worker advised me to declare myself bankrupt because of the amount of money I owed, but thank God I did not listen to this advice, as I would have been worse off in the long run. The debts I had on top of everything else knocked me back, so the social worker referred me to a woman's home in Purley. Sophia stayed with her other cousin's mum, as the Greens would not have her this time. I did not take it personally because it must have been hard to have the patience to understand that having depression is an illness that does not heal overnight. Many people believe all you need to do is pull yourself together; if only it was that easy. When you have been hurt and you're in pain, it can take a long time to heal, and many people do not have the patience to stay with you on the journey it takes to get there. If the shoe was on the other foot, I might have reacted the same way. Jason was not pleased when he heard I was going into the home in Purley either. He asked where Sophia was going to go the next time I had a breakdown. I replied that there was not going to be a next time. Hearing him say that made me more determined to get away from him and the dysfunction he brought into my life.

There were around fourteen of us in the home from different backgrounds, all different in age and race. Most days I had individual therapy, but it was group therapy that shocked me the most and proved an eye opener for me. Many of these women had been sexually abused in their childhood, and after hearing about their experiences, it made me realize how rife sexual abuse in society was. For all I was subjected to, I thank God that my dad never got me pregnant, as was the reality for some of the women there. Besides dealing with all the other issues sexual abuse had brought into their lives, then to have to go through the trauma of an abortion was absolutely devastating. It was heartbreaking to see women in their forties and fifties still trying to come to terms with childhood abuse that had taken such root in their lives. It inspired me that while I was still young enough, I still had the chance to try to overcome some of my insecurities before they determined my whole life. I listened intently to the advice given by the other women who had written themselves off as having no hope because they believed, as they were in later years of life, it was too late for freedom. But it is never too late.

I knew what I needed to do, but fear of the unknown kept me reverting back to my old behaviour. Fear keeps you in a dark place; fear keeps you from stepping out in faith to take that chance to experience life. Faith, hope, and belief are the keys that set you free. I was mad at myself for not being brave enough to step out of my comfort zone, which allowed me to keep making bad choices that kept sending me off the rails to the point of anxiousness and despair. I needed to gain control of my life but could not to do it by myself; only God could help me make a lasting change.

I left the home in Purley after two weeks, more determined than ever to get myself straight. I continued to have setbacks but felt stronger and started again to see Clara Metaxos fortnightly. This, along with my faith and determination, gave me the strength to fight on to make positive changes. Instead of focusing on trying to find love in all the wrong places, I channelled my energy into finding a good job. My job hunt was a success, and I started working at H.Samuels, the jewellers in April 2001, working at first twenty hours a week so that I could still pick up Sophia from school. I loved my job at H.Samuels because I love diamonds and jewellery, and I became one of their top sellers. I started to try to pay off all my debts, but it was hard, so I got a second job working at Superdrug's as a pharmacy assistant on Saturdays.

After six months of working two jobs, I approached the area manager of H.Samuels and asked him if there were any managerial positions in the area. Fortunately there was one position, but there were two drawbacks: one, the only supervisor position was in Camberley, which was far from my home, and two, it was full time, which meant I would not pick up Sophia after school for the time being. I weighed the options and decided I would take the job, as it would mean only working five days week in one job, not six days in two jobs. It was tough going, but I was more looking at the long-term prospect that if a supervisor role became available in a shop nearer to where I lived, I could apply for a transfer. Every day I got up at five thirty to leave at six thirty, drop Sophia to her aunt's, then get three trains from East Croydon to Clapham Junction, then change to get a train to Ascot, then change again to get to Camberley. The whole journey took around an hour and a half each way. Then on getting back to Croydon, I would get a bus to pick Sophia up from her aunt and uncle. Getting home at eight o'clock each night was exhausting, but it felt good to be able to have my own money to provide for Sophia and the opportunity to forge a career.

Being a single parent was not easy, but I handled it well, and I enjoyed spending time with my daughter. I took a great interest in her education and well-being, but Sophia had some behavioural problems in primary school, and I tried to support her in every way I could. I spent time talking to her teachers about what I could do as her mother at home to help with her education, and I attended all the parents' evenings, school plays, and most sports days by myself.

Sophia was a very bright child but lacked belief in her abilities, so I tried to reassure her by giving her encouragement all the time. I realised she probably picked up some of that unbelieving attitude from being around me, so I decided to dedicate a wall in her room to mark all her life achievements. I made a plaque called "Sophia's life achievements," and every certificate, acknowledgment of good behaviour that she had achieved since starting primary school, I stuck upon her wall. I wanted her to visually see all the great things she had done. I made reward charts to give her focus on finishing tasks and taught her how to cornrow hair and knit. We had such fun together, and we would dance and sing around the house; it was great. We had fun, but I was still strict, and I would discipline her when appropriate, if she misbehaved or was disrespectful. I was the main parent, as Jason's priorities were different. I am not saying he did not love her, but he could not seem to offer her the essential guidance she needed from a father. Jason gave money when he wanted to, but I always had to ask for it. I sensed he felt it gave him power having me come to him and ask for it, as it indicated I still needed something from him. It did not bother me, as he was her parent, and it was his responsibility to pay. He flitted in and out of her life when it suited him, and I was always the one he blamed for any reason. I always had to have done something to him for him to react the way he did—there was never any ownership from him for his own actions. It was hard for Sophia to understand, and she would get upset when he would break his promises to take her. Sometimes I would lie to her when he cancelled a visit and tell her he was working. I may not have been the perfect parent, but I tried to take responsibility for the problems my issues were causing.

I was achieving and experiencing so many new things in my life. I never thought I would amount to much, and although I still struggled with not liking myself, I could see good changes happening. It had been a while now since I had slept with any men, and it felt good. For the first time in my life, I felt I could make it and started believing I deserved to be treated better than I had been letting people treat me for so long, and that included the on-and-off intimate relationship with Jason. My feelings toward him started to die out the stronger I got. It was gradual, and I liken the process of removing him from my life as that of an addict weaning himself off a powerful drug. I had become obsessed over the years with making him love me and would wonder why he seemed to accept love from other women but was repulsed by the love I tried to show him.

Sometimes when I was in the midst of my unhappiness and insecurities, I would ask Sophia questions about Jason and his girlfriend when she would come back from visiting them. I am not proud of what I did then, but at the time, I thought if I could find out what she was like, it might help me to be the type of woman he would want to be with. I was screwed up already and knew this situation that had been going on for the last eight years of my life was killing me emotionally. The self-harming reached a new height every time he went back to whatever woman he was with, as it felt like rejection to me.

I remember asking God to give me the strength to dump him before he tossed me aside, and God, by his grace, allowed me the chance to leave him first. I pried his fingers off my life one by one, and it started with not allowing him around for dinner anymore; then I stopped the intimacy. When he would shout at me on the phone, instead of listening, I would just hang up. It got to the stage where there was no foothold for him in my life. I no longer desired what he had to offer . I wanted much more than the crumbs of so-called love he gave. It took eight years for my eyes to be opened to make the decision to cut all ties with him once and for all. For a long time, it felt like a vacuum had been left in my life mentally and emotionally—but not out of love; it was because I had grown used to the dysfunction and drama that being with him brought. I was an emotionally damaged woman who made unhealthy choices because of the abuse I experienced during my upbringing. At one point I was embarrassed and ashamed at how I acted over him and the things I allowed him to subject me to, in terms of his abusive behaviour, but now I embrace the lessons that the relationship taught me. I was a naive and damaged teenager when it all started, but in spite of it all, that relationship made me into a stronger woman. I learned that if a man really loved me the way I loved him, then his behaviour toward me would ultimately show love.

During this transitional period in my life, I was really lonely but never gave in to the temptation to indulge in my old destructive behaviour, as I was doing well. I was much stronger in myself and felt sure that I could remain in control of any situation that involved a man, so when I saw an acquaintance one afternoon in Croydon whom I had not seen in a couple of years who wanted to catch up, I did not see the harm. A few weekends later, he came round one with a bottle of wine. Sophia was at her cousin's house, so I had a drink. I was a little on edge at first, but after a while, I began to relax and made a point of telling him that I was not looking to get involved again. He said he only came round to see if I was okay, as he had heard that I was in the hospital a while back.

As the evening went on, I put on my old house tracksuit and came back downstairs. How I ever thought that this man, who I had slept with in another stage of my life, when I had no respect for myself, would honestly now treat me with any respect, I will never know. It did not take long for him to start trying to make moves on me, but I told him firmly and politely no. But he kept coming back stronger and stronger. In the end he raped me. I forced my elbow really hard into his neck and somehow managed to manoeuvre myself from under him and slid onto the wooden floor from the sofa. I screamed at him to get out of my house over and over again. He acted as if he had done nothing wrong and even had the cheek to ask what the matter was I asked him which part of "no" he had not understood. He could see I was distressed, so he left. I found the whole incident very traumatising, and I reported it to the police. I had to go through an examination at a rape suite situated in Denmark Hill in London and also gave a lengthy statement. The police took away certain items from my house for DNA testing, and they arrested and interviewed him.

In the end, due to the fact I had changed into my tracksuit during the course of the evening, the police said the prosecution could use this against me because it looked like I was comfortable enough with him to go and change my clothes. The police ended up registering his name and details of the allegation on their database, where it would remain for the next fifteen years. Should he be arrested again, it would show he had been arrested on suspicion of rape before. To be honest with you, I was angry about this, but who would really believe someone like me, a woman who had a colourful past with mental health issues? I had grown to accept that justice does not happen for people like me, so I learned to accept whatever unfair and hurtful situations I encountered in my life. The experience hurt me, but it could not break me any more than I was already broken. For a long time, I couldn't go outside without shaking and hated large crowds, as I believed people could see my shame and sadness.

A New Beginning

I attended a support group run through a church I briefly went to. It was for women, and I enjoyed going and mixing with like-minded women who loved God. I found it encouraging, but most of the time, I battled emotionally and spiritually between doing what was right by God and knowingly continuing to do what was wrong. When I looked at myself in the mirror, all I could see was a used and abused woman who was unlovable and disgusting. I tried to talk to God many times about how I felt, but I found it hard to find the words and felt too unclean to approach God most of the time. Due to my continuous struggle with negative behaviour, such as smoking cigarettes and self-harming, I did not think God would continue to love me, as I kept making so many mistakes. I desired to please him so much but felt that I was not acceptable and that my efforts were not good enough. Faith and belief are what please God, not trying to be someone that I am not to please him. He requires me to come as I am. I have learned, but it took a long time for it to sink in.

It had been over a year since the rape and a year and a half since I had been in any form of relationship with a man. I was very happy about this, as I had had enough of men. I had spoke to my ex-boyfriend Ryan a few times over the five years since we had broken up, but I sensed he was avoiding most of my calls, because the few times I called his house his mum would say he was out. Ryan was the only boyfriend I had who accepted me with all my faults and had always left a positive impression on me since we had a relationship all those years ago. I thought to myself that if I called him one more time and if he was not in, it would be the last time I called. Fortunately he came to the phone, and I asked him outright why he was avoiding my calls. Ryan, as always, told me the truth; he was not in a good place in his life and did not want me to know. I always respected his honesty. We talked frequently after that, and I told him what had been happening in my life. I was not scared of him but was scared of giving out any misleading signals, so I told him upfront I was not looking for a relationship with any man who was not a born-again Christian. He never once questioned my decision or asked me why. One day as I sat at home reading a book, Beulah Family Church, where I had briefly attended an Alpha course five years before, came into my thoughts. I had a vision of Ryan and me standing outside the church looking at a poster about Alpha on the notice board. Alpha was a group run by the church to help people who have questions about life. I sensed I was to take Ryan there, so a week later we met up and went down there to find out details. It was just like I pictured it, and they had a group starting the next week, so we signed up and went.

It lasted twelve weeks, and lots of different people from all different walks of life came. They had discussion groups on the meaning of life, God, Jesus, and topics to do with the Bible. It was a very informal atmosphere, and at first Ryan was apprehensive, but by week three, he felt comfortable. I never pressured him to go; he was genuinely interested in the discussions that took place, and a few months later, Ryan became a born-again Christian.

Ryan and I started to date again in 2003, and we spent a lot of time going out and doing fun things as a couple and also with Sophia. Sophia loved Ryan with all her heart and would always ask when he was coming round. Sophia was now nine years old, and although we had a good relationship, an element was missing for her, as she would talk about things she wished she could do with her dad. Ryan and

Sophia had a real father-and-daughter relationship, and it was so lovely to see. I underestimated how much she needed this bond in her life—a father who would consistently be there for her—and knew she was happy to have found it in Ryan. For the first few months, she just followed him wherever he went. But as time panned out, she felt secure enough to know he was not going to get bored of her and leave and she began to blossom in the confidence of knowing that. I saw a side to her that I had never seen before, a side that only surfaced with a father's love. We did mostly everything together: church, Bible group, restaurants, and theme parks, and even went on holiday together. When Ryan and I went on a date, Sophia would stay round her Aunt Pat and Uncle Donald's house or with Ryan's mum.

We attended the church where we went on the Alpha course, and I got baptised into my faith. For the first time in my life, I was experiencing real happiness and acceptance and no longer went out raving. I parted company with all of my old friends and cut all contact with the male acquaintances I used to keep. These people were never my friends, as they were only there when they wanted to go raving, or the men only wanted to use me, so it was no great loss because I had gained something much better and greater through God. I loved being with Ryan, and over the couple of years since we started dating again, I started to blossom into a woman I never knew existed. Ryan brought out the best in me and made me very happy. I still battled a lot of demons, and I found it hard to accept his love for me, but I was determined not to throw it all away this time.

Ryan worked hard as a manager for a retail store, and I worked at Halifax Bank in Battersea. I left H.Samuels in February 2003 after two years because my personal circumstances had changed and I needed a better income. I loved working there, as it gave me the drive and motivation I needed to believe that I could achieve great things career wise. I started as a cashier but was promoted two months later to a banking adviser.

Ryan and I planned to get married but had no idea as to how we should go about it. We went up to Hatton Garden in London to look at engagement rings, but I could not really make up my mind about the style I wanted. It was so exciting, and I was like a little child, telling anybody who would listen about the beautiful rings I saw.

Ryan told me a few days later he had a business lunch meeting he wanted me to attend with him to talk to potential new clients for the owner of his company. I was nervous and kept asking him what I should wear, but as ever, Ryan was laid-back and told me whatever I felt comfortable in. I was more nervous than he was! The meeting was in this nice bar called Mojamas in Croydon; the décor was suave and sophisticated, which was rare in this part of town. I was getting restless, as we had been waiting about twenty minutes already, and Ryan kept going up and down to the bar. One minute Ryan was standing in front of me, the next he was on his knees on the floor. I asked him what he was doing. As I tried to pull him up, the waiter brought over two glasses of champagne, and Ryan pulled out of his pocket this beautiful green velvet box, which contained a beautiful diamond engagement ring. Ryan asked me to marry him, and I said yes. There was never any business meeting; Ryan made it up so that I would not become suspicious as to why we were meeting in a wine bar in the middle of the day.

The date was set for the wedding July 23, 2005, and we told Sophia, who was extremely excited about being head flower girl. We had a small engagement party and told all our family and friends, who were very happy for us. We took our decision to get married very seriously, and we wanted to set a good example for Sophia. We attended a marriage guidance course that lasted six weeks with the pastor of our church and his wife. The marriage course looked at topics such as our upbringing, beliefs, and our family backgrounds, how we dealt with finances, children, and so forth. It was really informative, and I learned more about Ryan, which was good. I wanted to be a good wife to my husband, and I knew it would take a lifetime to achieve this, especially when both of us had not come from married households, so the course served as a taster as to what we should expect.

I found the wedding preparations really stressful, and I had no clue as to what colour dresses or flowers I wanted for bridesmaids. We did not have much money to get married and paid for it ourselves. Fortunately for us, God placed us in a church where people from all walks of life happened to have jobs or certain skills that could help us with our wedding. One lady was assistant manager of a wedding dress shop, another a florist, someone else's husband was a photographer; it was really a blessing, and I was touched by people's kindness. They never really knew us but went out of their way to help make sure we had a good wedding. When I first picked the colour for the bridesmaid dresses, I nearly made a fashion faux pas, as Pat suggested I pick peach. Luckily, I came to my senses! I lacked confidence in my decisions, even though I have a good fashion sense, and I ended up again during the planning of my wedding giving those involved too much control, which caused arguments. It was only toward the end of the preparations that I managed to gain control and to really start to assert my ideas.

The plan was always that my good friend at the time, Kimona, would ride in the wedding car with me on the day. I never thought about a man walking me down the aisle in place of my father as tradition commanded, because I did not have a father to do this. I had come to a place of forgiveness concerning my father a few years before, but I had no desire to resume any relationship with him. I invited my brother and sister to the wedding, but as I had not had a relationship with my mother since I was twenty-one, I did not invite her. Sophia's Aunt Pat suggested her husband Donald, so I asked him if he would give me away, and he said yes. It made perfect sense, as he was the nearest I had to a father figure at the time, but I just never naturally thought of asking him.

Six months later, on July 23, 2005, Ryan and I got married. It was a beautiful sunny day, and I couldn't sleep the night before. I was so nervous I got up at six in the morning and cleaned the kitchen windows! Before I knew it, it was time to go to the hairdressers to get my hair done, but she was running late, so that in turn made me late back to get ready. When I put my wedding dress on, it looked so beautiful and I felt like a princess. It was the first dress I had tried on when I went dress shopping, and I immediately knew it was the one. It was a strapless, A-line, champagne-coloured dress with pearls and embroidery on the bodice and all down the long train of the dress. As I stood looking in the mirror, I could not believe something so wonderful was about to happen for me. After so many years of heartache and despair, I had grown used to tears and disappointment. It was a strange feeling to be this happy, so naturally a part of me held back from being too overjoyed. Subconsciously it was built into my psyche like a protection barrier to always expect something bad. I hoped one day that barrier would be broken down. I had the most beautiful 1940s white Jaguar that I rode to the church with Donald in. I was already two hours late because of the hairdresser and nervous about standing in front of all those people, but when I walked up the aisle and saw Ryan, my fears melted away. I knew in my heart that we were meant to be together.

The service was a beautiful thanksgiving to God, and all the songs and words that were spoken fit in with what Ryan and I were about—love and commitment. The day went by so quickly, and my mouth hurt so much from the amount of smiling I was doing. The most poignant moment for me was when Sophia got up and spoke about how happy she was that I had married Ryan and that we had waited a long time for someone to come into our lives to be a family with us. I cried, because it was so true that Sophia and I had spent many nights praying and asking God to send a man to look after us. I was extremely proud of her and all the progress she had made; our lives were finally coming together.

It did not all go to plan, but in the end we were married, and that was the most important thing. We weren't due to go on our honeymoon to Paris until the next day, and as money was tight, we went back to our home. Ryan picked me up and carried me into the house. It was the most wonderful day of my life.

Ryan, Sophia, and I settled into family life quite easily, and Sophia called him "Dad" at times. I had never forced Sophia to call Ryan "Dad," but she had said that she would like to. I made it clear to her from the start that it was up her and that there was no pressure. Her own dad was still in and out of her life but noticed she was not as upset as she had been in the past. Contact between Jason and me had ceased, so she would ring him and he would tell her when he would take her. We had our ups and downs as a new family, as we were getting used to new boundaries and rules. I had been a single parent for nine years, so I struggled with my new standing in the family unit as God had shown it to be in his Word. Ryan never physically disciplined Sophia, but he grounded her if she misbehaved, and I supported him. Sometimes Sophia could see I found this hard and at times would try to play us against each other. But on the whole, there were more good times than bad as a family, and we achieved a good balance.

Three months later in November 2005 I became pregnant, and we were all elated. Sophia had been asking for a sister for a long time and constantly kept telling us she was praying about it. Being pregnant this time round was so much different, and I felt so much more grounded inside. I obviously knew it had a lot to do with how I had grown as a person and also due to a turn in life circumstances. We sat down with Sophia and told her that having this baby did not mean we would love her any less, but I explained that the baby would need extra attention. She understood as best as she could, but her main concern was if she could help bathe the baby.

In May 2006 I had some complications in the last trimester of my pregnancy, and there was a danger the baby was going to arrive too early. I was in and out of the hospital, and during this time, Sophia sometimes stayed at the Greens' house. On one such occasion, they rang and informed me that her dad had left her at the school until five o'clock in the evening, and on picking her up, he had hit her. This was not the first time he had left her at the school until late when he was meant to pick her up. But as much as I wanted to put a break on this relationship, some people's advice rang in my ears that Sophia would grow up hating me and that I should let her come to that conclusion herself. It was very hard to do this, as many times she came home unhappy from her visits. When her Aunt Pat told me, I felt like a complete and utter failure and became down. I did not want this continuous struggle with him affecting our lives anymore. I had managed to distance myself, but indirectly, through Sophia's continuing struggles with her dad, I kept being drawn in because she was my child, but I was helpless. On the advice of Jason's aunt and uncle, and after speaking to Sophia, Ryan and I decided to cut off contact between Jason and Sophia. It took Sophia a long time to repair from what she endured, and I could see how broken she was. All she ever wanted was to be her dad's number-one girl. Jason was not pleased about this decision, and the one and only time I accidentally picked up my home phone to a withheld number, he was on the other end of the line, demanding to know why Sophia had not told him how she felt and, as always, trying to hold me responsible. It had come as no surprise that even after not speaking to him in over a year how much anger he still displayed towards me, but I was not entertaining it. The short conversation ended with him mocking my husband and telling me I should go and do something degrading to my mother. He knew I was heavily pregnant but, as usual, wanted a reaction out of me. But I did not give one to him. I was determined that I was not going to let him ruin any more of my life, so I continued to focus on being healthy for the reminder of my pregnancy.

July 10, 2006, I gave birth to a beautiful baby girl called Esther. It was an easy birth, only six hours long, and she was not born early.

I settled into motherhood more easily the second time round and noticed much more than I had with my first child. I enjoyed spending time with my daughters. Donald and Pat were outside the room at the birth, and days later my husband voiced concerns about how much of an influence they had over my life. I could, in part, see his point, because at first during the labour, I wanted them in there more than I wanted my own husband. I had been married nearly a year and should have been by now starting to rely more on him instead of leaving him to the side. Ever since Donald became a qualified counsellor a few months before, I had also been paying him for counselling sessions. This continued after the birth of Esther for around six months, and Ryan also had a few sessions with him but no longer received any. I decided to continue to have counselling with him, as I was going through another low patch brought on by the incident with Sophia. I can see why he was concerned, and it is true that when you are in a situation that is close to you, you cannot see signs that something is wrong. I needed to figure out a way of pulling back, but I did not have to wait long, as circumstances eventually forced my hand.

Juggling being married with a new baby and a near teenager was hard at times and caused a few arguments between Ryan and me. There was so much pressure from all different angles, and now with the resurfacing of Jason in Sophia's life, it made things all the more difficult. When Esther was around six months old, Sophia saw her dad for the first time in nine months on her way walking home from school. He told her how much he missed her and how he was sorry for what he had done. When Sophia came home she told us what happened and said she wanted to give her dad another chance. I did not think this was a good idea, but Ryan and I decided to try to support her despite our reservations. In spite of all the obstacles Ryan and I faced, we were keen to get our family foundations right, so we got guidance from Sophia's Uncle Donald. He recommended that now we were married that Ryan be the main point of contact between Sophia and her dad and that when Sophia had any phone calls from her dad that Ryan remain in the room to monitor the calls. We also spoke about how to deal with the way Sophia wanted to play fight with Ryan and sit on his lap, as she saw how Ryan played with Esther and wanted to play that way as well. We tried to explain to her that the way Ryan played with Esther was not appropriate for her age, but I think she took it as rejection. We told him about the boundaries we set in the house—no walking around inappropriately, knocking before entering bedrooms, etc. He assured us that we were moving in the right direction. So my husband arranged to meet up with Jason before Sophia. It had been about nine months since they had last spent time together, and we were nervous as to how it would turn out. Ryan basically told Jason that if Sophia ever came home in a state again, the visits would be stopped and that he now was the main point of all contact between them. At first, Jason seemed to take it well, but soon enough he was pushing the boundaries by not dropping her back at agreed times. It seemed as though this situation would never get better, and combined with Sophia playing it up at times, it became stressful. I felt bad for my husband, as when we got married, he never thought he would have to put up with all this. Talk about baggage from hell!

She had a mobile we had given her so that she could receive phone calls from him, but this was abused, as he tried to arrange to meet with her without our knowledge. We were not party poopers. Sophia was more than welcome to see him, but the boundaries were there for her own good until the time was right. There was constant defiance to everything we had tried to set up, and God help us if she was grounded and it fell on one of his family parties. We had various members of his family ringing up and questioning our decision not to let her go, like they had a right to do this. Half of the time, they only surfaced when they wanted her to attend a family event. But we believed that if you were grounded, you could not go anywhere; it was part of teaching her that when she made bad choices, the consequences affected everything else. On a few occasions, Jason turned up at my door uninvited and even went to my husband's workplace on one occasion and threatened to kill him. My husband was never afraid of him but acted as a bigger person by refusing to be drawn into a confrontation with him. Ryan found it stressful being the go-between for Jason and Sophia to maintain contact, and it put an enormous strain on our marriage and my relationship with Sophia. I started to feel resentful, and at one time, it spilled into our relationship. I was angry and felt it was unfair. I had worked so hard to move on with my life. I was now married, trying to build a family, but a constant black cloud hung over me in the form of this situation. Again that ugly monster returned yet again—self-harming—and a couple of times, I ended up cutting. My husband knew about it and even cleaned me up. He tried his best to understand, but he found it extremely hard, and so the situation went on for months. I apologized to Sophia and asked her forgiveness for the times I took my frustrations with her dad out on her, and she forgave me, so we moved on.

I spent individual time with her and maintained our mother-and-daughter outings we had been doing since she was eight, going out once a month. We would go to the cinema and go to lunch or clothes shopping, and once a week for an hour, we would go to my bedroom, put on face masks, and file our nails and chat. Doing this stuff does not make me a great mother, but considering where I came from, I know I was a caring mother. Ryan and I helped her with homework, and every night I would tuck her in and say good night and sometimes even read her a story. Even though she was older, I enjoyed it, and I know she did as well.

Sophia was doing well educationally but had difficulty forming appropriate relationships within her peer group. Ryan and I had to go to the school a few times, and we would try to talk to her about being responsible, as there were always consequences. I tried everything and we had done everything, hoping and praying it would all turn out all right in regards to Sophia, but unfortunately she was heavily influenced by the wrong people. Sophia expressed an interest in talking to a counsellor, and I took this as a very positive step. It seemed that all the talks we had with her had started to sink in, and I noticed she was making a lot of effort. She had started dancing, and I took her along to auditions for different competitions. It was the first thing I had seen her so passionate about, and we encouraged it. Ryan and I would drop her to dance classes in Brixton and sit for an hour in the car to wait for her. I wanted her to be a success, to grasp all the opportunities given to her, and that included chances to express herself. So as her Uncle Donald ran a counselling agency, I asked him if he could arrange for Sophia to talk to someone on his book. We made it clear from the beginning how much we could afford, so I was taken aback when he suggested that I increase her sessions, as, according to him, the only way counselling would be effective was if she went every week. We were already paying forty pounds a fortnight, on top of childminders and bills, so there was no way we could pay 160 pounds a month for her counselling. I told him it was too expensive but sensed he was not happy with our decision. I sought outside advice from friends back at Beulah Church, who recommended that we go and see our doctor, who then made a referral to a counselling service for fourteen- to nineteen-year-olds called Off the Record. She started attending this free service weekly on the National Health Service.

The Green family had a huge role in my life. Their daughter Ingrid was a flower girl in my wedding, so it was natural that I asked Pat and her eldest daughter, Bridget, to be godmother for Esther. We had left Beulah Church a while back to go to the church where I became born again. Donald and his friend Kofi had now taken over as church ministers, as Pastor Richard and his family had left. Pastor Richard was popular with the congregation, and when he left, the majority went as well. The church now only consisted of Donald's family, Jason's mum, myself and Ryan, our children, and Kofi's family—fourteen of us in all. Donald performed the dedication service for Esther, and the day went well. It was small and intimate.

I found out Donald had approached Jason for money towards Sophia's counselling without our consent. I was disappointed, especially as, more than anybody, he knew all the stress that I had gone through with Jason. His behaviour was two-faced, and I could not understand why he would do this, as he never had a good word to say about his nephew. His explanation was that as Jason was not paying any money toward Sophia, he should be accountable, but he missed the point of why we were upset. It was not Donald's place to make that decision, and I was not approaching him as a family member who wanted to use his business service but as a paying client's mum. It was then, for the first time, I realised the boundaries were blurred in our relationship and could not see where it started and where it ended. Donald had been a father figure, my counsellor, and church minster rolled into one, and it was not healthy, so Ryan and I decided to leave a few weeks later and go back to Beulah Church. I had been gullible to think that the Greens would be loyal to me because blood, no matter how thin it is, is still thicker than water. I felt guilty for a long time about pulling away from them, as they had done a lot for me, but it was important for the health of my family to do this.

A few months later, in November 2007, I made contact with them, but the response I received was unwelcoming. Donald made it seem as though I was just using them when I was down, but nothing could have been further from the truth. They had been a major part of most events in my life and had seen me in good times and bad. The truth was that I had simply grown up and had become so much stronger; I was not the needy, lost little girl from care they once knew. I thought they would be happy for me, but Donald told me I had upset members of his family with my decision to have my space. He said although he understood my reasoning because he had given me counselling, others could not. I was mortified, as the last thing I ever wanted to do was upset anyone and in pulling away seemed I did more harm than good. I tried to apologize, and Ryan, on two occasions, went round to his house to discuss the situation with him on our behalf, but it was not enough. I also went round with Ryan on one occasion and noticed they had taken down all the pictures of my children and me on my wedding day with Donald. I was extremely upset.

We left it in their hands by saying when they were not upset with us, they should contact us. They made no attempt to do this, and I was surprised, because I thought these people loved me enough to want to sort it out. Donald said that when I told him we were taking a break, I never made it clear what I was taking a break from—the church or them. We had asked Pat at the time if we could meet with them before we left their church to tell them face-to-face, but they did not get back to me.

I said sorry many times, but we could not get past this situation, so the relationship waned. I constantly worried about the offence to the Greens on top of the other issues I was trying to deal with. I struggled to keep it together for my children, but I was dealing very well with not giving in to the temptation to cut myself, even though I was hurting inside and not liking myself very much. I would read Psalm 139 most days. It read:

O Lord you have searched me
and you know me.
You know when I sit and when I rise;
you perceive my thoughts from afar.
You discern my going out and my lying down;
you are familiar with all my ways.
Before a word is on my tongue
you know it completely, O Lord.
You hem me in–behind and before;
you have laid your hand upon me.
Such knowledge is too wonderful for me,
Too lofty for me to attain.

Where can I go from your spirit?
Where can I flee from your presence?
If I go up to the heavens, you are there;
If I make my bed in the depths, you are there.
If I rise on the wings of the dawn,
if I settle on the far side of the sea,
even there your hand will guide me,
your right hand will hold me fast.
If I say,"Surely the darkness will hide me
and the light become night around me,"
even the darkness will not be dark to you;
the night will shine like the day,
for darkness is as light to you.
For you created my inmost being;
you knit me together in my mother's womb.
I praise you because I am fearfully and wonderfully made;
Your works are wonderful,
I know that full well.
My frame was not hidden from you
when I was made in the secret place.
When I was woven together in the depths
of the earth,
your eyes saw my unformed body.
All the days ordained for me
were written in your book
before one of them came to be.
How precious to me are your thoughts, O God!
How vast is the sum of them!
Were I to count them,
they would outnumber the grains of sand.
When I awake,
I am still with you.
If only you would slay the wicked,
O God!
Away from me, you bloodthirsty men!
They speak of you with evil intent;
your adversaries misuse your name.

Do I not hate those who hate you, O Lord,
and abhor those who rise up against you?
I have nothing but hatred for them;
I count them my enemies.
Search me, O God, and know my heart;
test me and know my anxious thoughts.
See if there is any offensive way in me,
And lead me in the way everlasting.

I tried to make a conscious effort to look in the mirror each day and tell myself that I loved me. I was hoping that, although I never felt it, soon enough my soul would hear the positive affirmations I was giving myself and start to believe it. It was hard to speak to anybody about the continuing negativity I battled with about myself, especially as God blessed me with so much: a loving husband, successful career, and two beautiful children. I was mentally stuck in a maze and would not allow myself to enjoy this period in my life, constantly blaming myself for other people's actions toward me. I was broken-hearted about my past and still hurting badly about what happened as a child. I had become a slave to sadness and despair. Even though I physically was no longer in that place, I was still there emotionally and spiritually. God had moved me to a place of hope and promise, a new start with my husband and my family, but I needed a spiritual breakthrough, which would then filter through to my mentality. I began to read my Bible regularly and prayed, hoping this would pave the way for a permanent change.

I had not seen my brother and sister much over the years, as our relationship was strained due to our childhood, which caused a lot of accusations and pain for us, so it was not worth the bother. I saw my brother more than my sister, and even then, it was not much. My brother told me he had found an auntie of ours who I had heard about as a child but never met. I grew up in a very secretive family and only ever vaguely remembered meeting other family members once. We were very young, and our parents took us to a family barbeque in Balham on a hot, sunny day. I remember calypso music playing and the smell of jerk chicken, doing limbo under a rope, and everyone having fun and taking turns. It was before I was sexually abused, and I remember that because I was happy and not self-conscious. I wondered over the years as we grew up why we did not have any family round, as, according to Mum, we came from a big family. Our questions were never answered, and we came to accept that our family was just the five of us.

My brother found out the real reason during a conversation with Auntie Rose, who asked my brother who his father was. Our dad was in a relationship with my nan first, and she was shocked to hear that her cousin Cookie, our mum, had a relationship that produced three children with him. According to my aunt, her and Mum were close growing up in Jamaica when they were young; then one day Mum vanished and she never saw her again. She also told him that our dad and Nan had been offering Obeah services while they were in Jamaica. Obeah is a form of voodoo practised in the West Indian regions and is evil, more known in broader society as witchcraft.

Apparently our dad and Nan took payment for these services but ended up running off with their clients' money. People were after them, hence the reason for not keeping in touch with relatives and the secrecy. Now, thinking back to the weird practices we endured at home, such as the bags of hair Mum kept every time she combed our heads, the blue bathwater baths to keep evil spirits away, and having the seats cut out of our knickers, made sense. I was disgusted to hear this, but in all honesty, it made no difference to me. Had I heard this news five years ago, it would have probably devastated me. When I caught my dad in bed with my nan, I was subjected to a beating, made to look like a liar and troublemaker, but it was the truth. I need not have told Mum, as she already knew, and it is quite sickening to think they were happy to live like this—drowning in all the secrets and lies that my dad created through an atmosphere of fear. He was happy to work his way sexually through the female generations—Nan, Mum, and then me—and I believe he would not have stopped if I did not have the courage to speak out against him. It was as if he believed all the females in the family were his for the taking, and God only knows if he has abused any other girls. As a survivor of incest, I can now see that his treatment of me was not personal but more to do with satisfying his sick urges. According to Mum, it was normal for Jamaican fathers to come into the bathroom when their daughter is washing and intimately examine them, so his behaviour, in their eyes, was normal. Still, I had gotten to the point of forgiving him and my mum a long time ago and have only started recently to pray that God can bring them to a place of repentance for their actions.

It took longer for me to forgive my mum, and I believe this was because when I became a mother of a daughter and felt the love I had for Sophia, I could not understand why she never did more to protect me. I have seen her now and again over the years out and about in Croydon and was shocked at how worn out and stressed she looked. Mum looks like a woman who has no peace. Despite whatever went on in Mum's life, she always appeared to look healthy and well. Even some of the shine she took in maintaining her appearance was clearly gone. Whenever I used to see her, she was always uncomfortable acknowledging or talking to me. I used to take this as a personal rejection, which would make me cry and send me into a depression that would last for weeks. But the last time I saw her, a day before my thirty-second birthday on the eighteenth of August 2008, my heart filled with compassion toward her. Who knows what my mum had to endure earlier in her life that made her make the decisions she chose. She has lost a lot because of her choices. Out of three children she has given birth to, only one, my younger sister, talks to her.

She had lost out on a relationship with Sophia and has never met her other grandchild, Esther. It cannot be easy living with so many terrible memories and secrets on your conscience. Our conversation did not last long, but she asked if I was still going church, and I told her yes, I was still a Christian. She was surprised, but what is telling is the few times I have seen her has been at major stages of my life. I saw her after my nervous breakdown, when I became a Christian, and after I married. Maybe God was using these times as a testimony to her that the fear and control that she lives under can be broken and that nothing bad will happen to her if she steps out, because I was still living and being blessed in spite of Dad's threats of me going deaf and blind for speaking out.

I hope one day my mum will gain the courage to leave. Fear will never overcome truth, but the faith to believe this may be hard for her, as she has lived like this for so long. My prayer for her is that she will experience peace and life in Christ before she dies. On parting with her, she wished me a happy birthday. I walked away feeling taken aback but glad that she remembered.

Betrayal

I looked at the clock. It was 4:40. School finished at 3:30, so I was wondering why Sophia was not home yet, as she was supposed to be home by 4:10. She had no dance practice or any after-school events, so she should have been back by now. It was not as if she was coming from far; school was only twenty minutes away.

Before the latest incident last night everything seemed to be going well in terms of her behaviour, and over the last few months, we had grown closer in our relationship and as a family. The holiday we had just come back from in Cyprus was really fun, apart from one incident where she tried to get involved when Ryan was talking to Esther; she was disrespectful, so Ryan told her off. That was my main concern at times—her attitude toward us. Typical teenager. If everything was going her way, she was nice as pie, but if you told her off or reminded her off her responsibilities, which at times as parents we have to do, she would sulk.

The night before, we had let her go to a friend's birthday party. This was on a Sunday October 5, 2008. My husband was hesitant about letting her go at first, but because I said we should trust her to go, he allowed it. We dropped her off and reminded her of what we expected—good behaviour and for her to be out on time for us to pick her up. When we returned she was not outside, and my husband ended up having to go in to get her. She was nearly ten minutes late. Her excuse was she did not have a watch, so we asked her why she did not ask her friends for the time. Sophia did not answer. So she was grounded.

You might think, *Big deal she came out ten minutes late*, but it was the principle. Again and again Sophia was given many chances in whatever situation to operate within the boundaries set. For example, she would arrive home late from school, so we asked her what time she thought she could reach home. She said four ten, so she helped set her own boundaries but had trouble sticking to them.

I had been lying down on my bed for about ten minutes when I had heard the house phone ring. Ryan came upstairs and told me that the deputy head of Sophia's school had rung, wanting to speak to me, and that when he asked if he could take a message, he did not want to leave one with him. Immediately in my spirit I knew something was wrong and thought maybe this boy Sophia had told me had been harassing her had troubled her, as a few weeks earlier. I rang back the school and was put through to the deputy head, who, when I asked him where Sophia was, wanted to know if I was in the room by myself. I asked him why, and he asked me a couple of times if I was sitting down.

He then told me that Sophia had come to school and in an afternoon lesson told a teacher that my husband was sexually abusing her. I fell to the floor screaming, "No, what she is saying is not true."

Ryan kept asking what was wrong. I could only just make out what the teacher said would happen next, which was that they had reported it to social services and that I had to arrange a place for Sophia to stay. I cannot explain to you how devastating hearing this was. I went from crying hysterically to numbness. I asked the teacher if I could have time to make other arrangements, and he said he would call back in twenty minutes.

I then broke the news to Ryan, who just sat on the chair crying with Esther in his hands. Panic set in, and I racked my brains for someone Sophia could stay with. She had told the deputy head she wanted to go and stay with Donald and Pat Green, but I was determined that was not going to happen, as I believed the situation would be made worse by them, as they thrived off drama and up until this point Sophia had not wanted to see them. We had encouraged her to ring them in the past, but she said their daughter Ingrid had been mean to her at school and had no interest in making contact.

Our friends William and Caroline Seymour from our church came into my mind, so I rang their house. Caroline was a schoolteacher and had just stepped in from school. I tried to explain to her what had happened, but I was not making any sense. I eventually managed to ask her if she could keep Sophia for the night until this situation was sorted out. She agreed and went down to the school to pick her up. It was sheer pandemonium in our house, as our mobile phones were ringing nonstop, but Ryan sat there glued to the seat in shock. Our pastor from Beulah Church and Ryan's sister, Cheryl, to name a few, had by now picked up the messages and were ringing to find out what was going on.

The house phone also rang. It was Sophia's Aunt Pat, who I had not heard from in nine months. She asked me if I was okay, and at first I lied and said yes, but then I broke down in tears and told her what Sophia had said. She said she already knew, as her daughter Ingrid, who went to the same school as Sophia, came home and told her. It had not even been twenty minutes since we got the call from the school, and I immediately became suspicious of her call.

According to Pat, Sophia had broken the news to Ingrid that morning in school break, and she was ringing to ask where Sophia was. She then said, "Imagine what Jason would do if he found out." Her tone was that of someone salivating at the prospect of that encounter. A discussion I had with her a year earlier came to mind, in which she had said that Sophia had been telling her daughters she was upset about being at home. At the time I asked her what was said, but Pat did not want to tell me. I brought up this conversation again, hoping she would tell me in light of the current situation, but she deflected answering. I was so angry and upset. I decided I did not want to speak on the phone to her any longer, so I hung up.

As I put down one phone, another would ring. The deputy head was now ringing back for the third time and, to his credit, was very patient and understanding as I tried to get through to my friend Caroline about Sophia. Relieved, I gave him the news that she would be coming to take her. Then I started panicking about Esther, running around like a headless chicken as I flung clothes into a suitcase, screaming at Ryan that we had to take her down to his mum's house until this was all over, which seemed to rouse him out of his shocked state.

I thought that because of the nature of the allegations, social services would come knocking any minute to take Esther away. I remembered back to when my dad had sexually abused me. Social workers and police were all over my house, so the whole experience became real for me once again. We drove most of the journey to my mum-in-law's in silence, and I drifted away into my thoughts. It felt like I was in the twilight zone, and I tried to convince myself that this was a nightmare and soon I would wake up and everything would be back to normal. How could the same set of circumstances I faced as a child come back to visit me? I knew deep in my heart these allegations were not true and, after having so many years of heartache and pain from the sexual abuse I suffered in my childhood, that my God would never give me a husband who would do that to my kids because he knew better than anybody how much I had endured.

I did not know why this was happening, but I was certain that God would help us through, no matter what we would have to face. I swung between different emotions during the car ride to Ryan's mum's house in Battersea, and by the time we arrived, I was very angry and had even sworn a few times. I was outraged that Sophia would do this to us; it was as though she had it all planned out with no thought of the damage she was doing to us or her little sister, Esther. I knew the authorities would not see it like this, as they had a duty to investigate every allegation. Rightly so, for the children who, like me, needed that help after such a traumatic event, but not for children who just wanted to get their own selfish needs met.

It was late by the time we got back to our house, and we were not even tired. We deliberately got back late, as we could not face going back home. I had already hated my house in Hood Close Croydon for a long time and dreamt for so long about leaving. We were waiting for a reply on a house that we had applied for in another area but had been waiting so long we thought it would not go through. Hood Close had been my second home since living the care system, but what started out as a fresh start after I had the nervous breakdown became a constant depressing reminder of the bad times I had faced. I had lived here for eight years and had been raped, physically assaulted, and had bad arguments in this house. When Ryan moved in after we got married, I thought it would be a better place for me. We decorated the whole house with great enthusiasm, but after a while the new coat of paint could not take away the bad memories, and now we had to deal with another bad situation; it was so unfair.

That night we could not sleep, as we were both so anxious about the next day. We discussed every possible scenario, but it was all just guesswork, based upon my recollection of events from young. Ryan's sister called and told us she was going to find Ryan a solicitor; then she prayed with us. That was the only good thing to come out of this sorry tale—it taught Ryan and me to pray like we had never done before. As we prayed, Psalm 71 came to mind. It partly read:

> In you Lord, I have taken refuge; Let me never be put to shame. Rescue me and deliver me in your righteousness; Turn your ear to me and save me. Be my rock of refuge, to which I can always go; Give the command to save me, For you are my rock and my fortress. Deliver me, O my god from the hand of the wicked, From the grasp of evil and cruel men. For you have been my hope O Sovereign lord, my confidence since my youth. From my birth I have relied on you; You brought me forth from my mother's womb, I will ever praise you. I

> have become like a portent to many, but you are my strong refuge. My mouth is filled with your praise all day long. Do not cast me away when I am old; do not forsake me when my strength is gone. For my enemies speak against me; those who wait to kill me conspire together. They say "God has forsaken him; pursue him and seize him, No one will rescue him." Be not far from me O God; Come quickly, O my God, to help me. May my accusers perish in shame; May those who want to harm me be covered with scorn and disgrace.

After we read, Ryan and I held each other and cried. Eventually Ryan fell asleep, but I went downstairs and tried to watch TV. I could not sleep; all I could do was cry. I racked my brains for reasons as to why Sophia would do this to us, to me, but nothing could prepare us for what was to come.

The morning light shone through the blinds, as I had forgotten to close them the night before. It felt like only a second since I had fallen asleep, and within minutes the phone started to ring. Ryan answered the phone. It was his sister, Cheryl, calling to see if we had heard any further news, which we had not. We had not eaten since the day before, but I was not hungry. My stomach ached, but they were not hunger pangs; it felt as though someone had their hands pulling and wringing my stomach at the same time. Ryan and I said very little to each other, as we were both lost in our own worlds.

Diagnosis Murder was on the TV, which was one of my favourite shows, but I could not concentrate on watching it. I lay there with tears running down my cheeks. My world had come to an end, and I never saw this coming with Sophia. What was odd was that it came at a time where our relationship was very close. She and Ryan had always had a close relationship; she even went to work with him most Saturdays to earn extra pocket money; it did not make any sense. We had to go into Croydon to put some money in the bank, as some bills were due to come out, but we did not want to face outside. It took us an hour to coax ourselves out of the house, and as we walked through Croydon, we held each other's hands tightly. We felt ashamed and embarrassed by what Sophia accused Ryan of and vulnerable and paranoid that people were staring at us as if they knew the allegations we were facing.

I rang Social Services to find out what was happening, explaining to the social worker what we were told by the deputy head of Sophia's school. Her tone was suspicious, and she gave vague details about when we would be contacted. I had never met this woman before, yet she had already judged us like I had done wrong. I was just told to go home and wait to be contacted, as the police were now informed and would be coming round to see us with a social worker. While I was on the phone, call waiting continuously beeped; it was Sophia's Aunt Pat. I could not even think, let alone answer her calls, and I did not feel comfortable talking to her, especially since her first call the day before. She resorted to texting, asking if I wanted any help and saying the company she worked for could get me a solicitor. I did not answer her texts.

When we arrived back home, our neighbour told us that the night before when we were at my mum-in-law's house, the police were knocking on our door. We asked her if they said anything, and she said they had a call that a disturbance was coming from our address and that a woman was in the back of the car. When we got back in the house, I started crying hysterically. It was no coincidence that they had come round. We had never had police knock our house for anything to do with us; only a couple of times when Sophia's friend ran away from home they came to see if she was here.

We had not been back ten minutes when the social worker and a detective constable from the child protection unit knocked. After the formalities, the DC asked my husband to go upstairs, as they wanted to talk to me alone. The social worker did all the talking, and I found out many things that day I was not aware of, like how Sophia had been seeing her dad secretly, despite us asking her if she wanted to see him on many occasions. She insisted she did not. Apparently she had seen him three times since Christmas 2007, which was when she decided she did not want a relationship with him anymore, as she said he had upset her. She had gone to his flat in South Norwood on one occasion the day before my birthday. I allowed her to go and sleep over at her best friend's house, which she had done many times, but she used this as an opportunity to go round his house. She had said she was frightened of him many times, so I did not understand why she had done this. We only stepped in after that Christmas and said to her that she was not allowed to see him anymore for the time being, due to what she said she experienced.

Imagine what it was like for the last nine years seeing your child upset all the time by situations she said been caused, and I experienced most of them with her dad. It was painful. Sophia said I had stopped her seeing her family, which again was more lies. She chose not to see or ring them. Sophia never made any effort to ring them, and it was the same with her family. She was fourteen; should I not help her to be independent? I could not force her to see her family, and as far as we knew, it all stemmed from the argument with her cousin that she did not want me involved with. They sat on the sofas, and I sat on a dining room chair opposite them. The conversation felt like an interrogation. The social worker told me that Sophia had said the touching had been going on for a year and that Ryan would come in her and Esther's room at bedtime and touch her breast under her top as Esther sat in the cot. She asked me if I believed this was going on, and I cried "No" over and over again and said that my husband would never do that to her. The social worked replied stiffly that in most cases the mothers never believed their partner would abuse their child, but then, when the partner is arrested and questioned, they admit it. I repeated again that this was not true and told them I was abused as a child and there was no way, with the despair I had had to endure, that I would ever let that happen to my child. I told them that I had told Sophia about six months ago what had happened to me, as she asked why I never had a dad and why was I in care homes. I never went into the gritty details. I only told her in a matter-of-fact way: I was abused by my dad for a number of years and that I was taken into the care system. I could have hidden this from her and continued to avoid telling her the truth, but I wanted to be honest. I gave them examples of how careful I was with Sophia and how Ryan never went in her room without knocking. When Sophia went to bed, she would come down to let Ryan check her school diary and say good night to him. Then I would go up and tuck her in. It may seem strange to a lot of people that I was still tucking in my fourteen-year-old daughter at night, but she liked to have her back rubbed, and sometimes I would still read her a story and pray with her. I did not mind doing this, but even that she turned round and used against me, telling them I treated her like a child in doing this, like I was doing it against her will.

Many people probably wonder how I can be so sure that he was not abusing her, and to be honest, it does not surprise me that people think like this, because we live in a cynical and evil world. Many think there is no smoke without fire, but I know with every beat of my heart—I'm even willing to lay my life on what I believe—that my husband never did this terrible thing he was accused of. If you saw them together through all the years we had been a family, how she looked up to him, how he nurtured and looked after her, you would know. More importantly, I know God knows, but I did not understand why this had to happen. Again she asked how I was sure, and I replied I just knew in my heart it was not true.

You know when you cry so much that it turns into such deep-wrenching sobs that you cannot catch your breath and your ribs hurt? That's how I cried. In all my life I never thought I could go through any deeper pain as I went through with the abuse and rejection. I was wrong. There was another depth to pain, lower than hitting the floor, a level beyond, which came in the form of betrayal from my own child. After a while the sobbing stopped, and a strange quietness came over me. I spaced out and went to another place inside my head. I had done this since a child when my dad abused me. I would become detached from myself; it was my way of dealing with the pain, like going into a daydream, but in the daydream I was just wandering around in nothingness. The social worker continued to bombard me with questions and revelations at the same time, and I was expected to have answers straightaway while in my mind trying to come to terms with her betrayal. I clearly had underestimated my own daughter. This social worker asked me if I would get a divorce and whether I would ask my husband to move out while this was being investigated. How ridiculous was she to ask such questions and expect answers instantly. I had been married to Ryan for nearly four years, and there was no way I would divorce him; he had done nothing wrong. This has been my experience of social workers: They cannot empathise or humanise any situation. All anyone's life is to them is an exercise of dismantle and destroy, looking for fast results so they can move on to the next case quickly. For her to ask this so flippantly proved this.

She then asked me if I would have my daughter back home. I said no. Then she asked, "Even if she was telling the truth?" and again I said no. By this point my heart had hardened and I had become so numb that I blanked out under immense pressure and stress. By the end I said no to every question she asked and told her I would not say anything more without a solicitor. She told me that Sophia had said she would not come back home even if Ryan left. She was trying to catch me out, and little did I know that one comment about not having her back home would be taken out of context of the pressure I was under and become used as everyone's weapon against me. While I understand she had a job to do, I did not appreciate her bullish tactics; she was relentless. It could not have happened at a worse time because all over the news, the case about Baby P, who died because of physical abuse was huge, and social services was under immense scrutiny because they had failed this baby. I resigned myself to the fact that there was nothing I could say or do to stop this process happening, and I felt vulnerable, depressed, and defeated all at the same time. My mind wandered to what Ryan was doing upstairs. I really wanted him down here to help me get through this, just to sit and hold my hand, but he was under suspicion with them. But to me, he was the only family I had and the only person I truly trusted. The police woman asked me every so often if I was all right, as she could see I was distressed. She only asked me a couple of questions, one which was of particular interest—how long ago did I tell Sophia I was abused.

Finally the questioning came to an end, and I was told Sophia wanted to press charges. But when they told her she would have to do a full video statement, she did not want to do it. It was explained to her that in order to move forward with the case, this was the procedure, so they were going to try again tomorrow. I was told to call my husband back downstairs so they could talk him, and when he came down, the DC also told him what would happen next. The DC mentioned to him that I was not allowed to discuss the conversation that had just taken place and that he must not ask me. On leaving, the social worker told me she would be in touch. I felt sick and crushed by what I had just gone through and did not know what to say to Ryan. I had just exposed a private part of myself to strangers, yet I could not share this with my husband. I could see the pain in his eyes as he searched mine, looking for a sign that it would be all right and that an end was in sight. But he could tell by the vacant look my eyes portrayed that this was not so.

Why was life so against me? All I had ever done was try to overcome the devastation other people had caused and make a go of the remains of my life I had left, even though for nearly all of it, I had thought there was no point, as I hated life. I dared to believe when Ryan and I married that it would be the start of many great adventures for us as a family, something Ryan and I really wanted, as both of us had to deal with difficult but different circumstances growing up. I had managed for the last few years, with help and encouragement from my church and faith, to get my paranoia about being born cursed under control, but this situation blew it back up so crazily. It affirmed to me this was definitely true—I was cursed. I wanted to act out in rebellion against God, so I got on my coat, threw my hood on my head, and walked out of the house to the shop, crying openly walking along. I brought cigarettes and a bottle of vodka, and Ryan walked beside me, trying to encourage me not to smoke because since being baptised, I had not touched them. I did not care what he had to say and walked straight into the road without looking. Secretly I hoped a lorry would strike me down, as my life was certainly over. I crossed the road and fell to my knees on the muddy pavement, not caring who saw the state I was in. I began shouting over and over that my life was finished, asking God to kill me, to end my life. I wanted to be under the dirt that I was kneeling in. I had had enough. I could not see past today, let alone tomorrow. Ryan tried to tell me that he and Esther needed me and that we would make it through, but I felt they were better off without me, a woman cursed with much misfortune.

The phone continued to ring nonstop, and Ryan's sister, Cheryl, had now found a solicitor for him. We also found out through the solicitor that my husband should not have been sent upstairs while they were questioning me. Cheryl had some contacts through her church that were high up in the social services, and she went to them to find out about their procedures. Cheryl worked so tirelessly on our behalf, dealing with all the legal aspects, finding out our rights, phone calls, letters, speaking to different authorities. She was a real godsend, and I do not know how we would have coped without her.

Ryan was trying to deal with the phone calls while I descended into despair, smoking cigarettes and drinking vodka and orange juice on an empty stomach at two o'clock in the afternoon. I had not smoked cigarettes in five years, and the taste was repulsive, so the smoking ended as soon as it started. I only smoked a few cigarettes before Ryan took the packed off me.

Ryan made me a cheese toasty for me to eat, but I refused. The vodka went to my head very quickly, as I had not eaten in two days because I was anxious. Ryan actually had to open my mouth and encourage me to bite it, as he was concerned about the effect the alcohol was having. I only managed a couple of bites and wanted to continue to drink, but Ryan took the rest of the alcohol and threw it down the sink. The social worker who had interviewed me a few hours earlier called back and told me they would not be pursuing a case against my husband. When I asked why, she said they had checked out some information but would ring me to officially confirm tomorrow. She said she could understand why I would not want Sophia back home after what she had done but that I should have her back and show her tough love. I explained that both my husband and I had tried in so many ways, but what else could we do? There is only so much you can do as a parent, and she agreed.

DC Romeria from the police child protection team rang to tell us she was assigned to the case. She confirmed the police would not want to question or interview my husband and that she would call me later in the week to tell me the outcome of Sophia's interview.

It had only been three days since this situation blew up, but it felt like a lifetime. One day blurred into another, and although the case was not being carried forward, it did not bring any relief for us. The comments Sophia had made about us and the revelations that came to light spun round and round in my head.

I was signed off work for six months due to depression and could not face going back . The doctor convinced me not to make any hasty decisions and said that I would feel better for doing this. He also referred me to a cognitive therapist to help me with my self-esteem, which had hit an all-time low. I was disappointed with myself, as I thought I was done with therapy. To me, going back was a sign that I had not made any progress. It reminded me of the twelve years on and off when I was in and out of different therapies, trying to find out who I was. Still, I accepted the doctor's advice and was told that there was a three-month waiting list. The doctor wanted to put me back on antidepressants, but I firmly refused, as they made me feel like a walking zombie. All the time this was going on, I still had to function as a mother. In the evenings Ryan and I would drive down to Battersea to spend time with Esther and fill his family in on the day's events. Then we would come back to our friends at Beulah Family Church who were calling to pray with us and offer support. They rallied around us in any way they could and were a tower of strength during these trying times. Sophia's school rang, asking when I would make the first payment for her trip to Paris, unaware of the latest developments that had been going on. She was meant to go to Paris as part of a student music exchange for which we had given her permission to go as recognition for improvement in her behaviour. I informed the teacher she was no longer going, as she had not behaved. I was not going to reward her behaviour, as this would send out the wrong message. The trip cost two hundred pounds, and I could not justify spending that money at this point.

A letter came through about her day surgery for a minor foot operation, which I tried my best to get sorted out by ringing the hospital. The date for the operation was two weeks away, and I tried to explain to them that there had been a serious family situation and that my daughter was not living with me at the moment. I asked if they could put back the date by a few weeks, as we were not sure where she would be living, but they told me this was not possible, as they had other patients waiting for a date. I was told by the receptionist that whenever the situation was sorted out, all we would have to do was go back to the GP, who would refer her back. Then she would have only to wait two weeks for the operation, as she had seen a consultant and had an x-ray already, so I agreed to that option.

It was like juggling ten balls at once, and I constantly kept breaking down in tears. Ryan and I continued to support each other but found it hard to convey what we felt. I stayed in bed most of the time, crying under my duvet, but on other days, I felt anger and disgust at what Sophia had done to us. She had not shown any inkling that she was sad and unhappy living with us, and only two days before this happened, she told me that when she grew up she wanted to be like me. I was touched by her compliment, as I did not recognise myself as someone to look up to. I could get angry and anxious at times around and with her, but she obviously saw something good about me. If she had run away, as upsetting and sad as it would be, it would have been easier to accept and easier to work through than the lies she had chosen to tell to destroy us as a family. We could have gotten help and support in working out the issues that were affecting her. I thought back and remembered when I was a single mother the nights Sophia and I cried, asking God to bring someone good into our lives to look after us; it was unreal how it had all panned out now.

Rage took over me as I stood in her room looking at the wall of achievement I had spent seven years building up. In seconds I ripped down every single certificate that hung on the wall. The many great things I had tried to help Sophia achieve from a young child, all the time and effort I had put in as a single mum and with Ryan as a family had been a waste of time.

I rang the family rights group, which was a voluntary organisation that consisted of social workers, family solicitors, and support workers who gave advice to families who had social services involved in their lives, and I was shocked to find out from the adviser that the situation we found ourselves in was far from abnormal. Many children were making these types of allegations against their parents concerning physical or sexual abuse. It gave me little comfort knowing these facts, but I remembered back to when Sophia's old best friend, the one where the police kept knocking our door every time she disappeared, had done this exact thing—accusing her dad of physical abuse, which resulted in her living in a care home, doing exactly what she wanted to do. According to the adviser, this boiled down to children wanting to have their own way, not wanting boundaries or rules. These were cases where children were not put on a child protection register nor had any social service involvement after the initial investigation.

Thursday, October 9, 2008, had finally arrived and was a day of extreme anxiousness for not only Ryan and me, but for our friends and family, as this was the day we would find out what would be happening with the police investigation. Everyone was praying for us, but I found it hard to pray with so many things going round in my mind. So I stayed in bed. Finally DC Romeria called and told us officially that the police would not be looking to go any further with the case due to inconsistent information given by Sophia. She wanted to come round to discuss with me her interview that afternoon, so we waited.

Our pastor from our church also came round to offer us support, and shortly after he arrived, DC Romeria came. The four of us sat in the front room, and DC Romeria told us that they had tried to arrange an interview with Sophia yesterday, but she was still not committing to doing it, so finally she made a decision for a duty social worker to accompany her so that she could be interviewed. When Sophia was interviewed by DC Romeria, she spent nearly the whole time complaining about the amount of chores and responsibility she had at home. DC Romeria pointed out to her that this was perfectly normal and was part of preparing her for own independence. Only toward the end, when DC Romeria asked about the allegations she had made, did she want to talk about it. What she said was full-scale touching under her top on Monday had now three days later become tickling her under her armpit, which, DC Romeria rightly pointed out, were two completely different things. When DC Romeria expressed to her the implications of her initial allegations—that Esther could be taken away and Ryan put in prison—Sophia was unfazed by the consequences and hell-bent on pressing charges. So based on the interview and other information gathered, they were not looking to make a case against Ryan.

DC Romeria asked me if I ever hit Sophia, and I replied yes. Sophia had mentioned an incident two years before, and because of this, DC Romeria said I would have an entry against my name for unnecessary chastening of a child. Hearing the things she said about me in the interview brought me again to tears. I was supposed to be feeling elated at hearing the news that Ryan had nothing to answer for, but I was in pain. I was mentally troubled.

While the DC was still there, I received a call from a social worker from Social Services, called Maria La Rue, who had just been assigned to Sophia's case. Maria spoke with an accent I had never heard before, and when asked, she told me she was from Albania. She was an agency social worker who had only been working in London for a few months. The reason for her call was she wanted to drop off Sophia back at home that afternoon but also said that Sophia had made it clear she wanted to go and live with her Aunt Pat and Uncle Donald. I told her that I would need to get advice and asked if she could call back, and as DC Romeria was still at my house, I asked her. She was very clear that if Sophia came back home without any proper support from social services, the likelihood was that she would make these allegations again. She explained that while it was on her file, the outcome of this case, they were required by law to treat every allegation as new, which meant if she did it again, we would have to go through this again. She was also concerned about how she would be around her sister, as she said Sophia seemed to harbour resentment towards her. We asked her what help we could get, and she told us about CAHMS, an organisation that worked with young people with mental health issues, and Oak Avenue, which offered mediation for young people and their families. Cheryl, Ryan's sister, rang and spoke to DC Romeria about the outcome of the police case and the options available to us. After much discussion we told Cheryl what we decided, as I had given third party authorisation for her to speak on our behalf to Maria La Rue. She relayed the decision—that until we had support from social services in form of family mediation and counselling for Sophia, she could not come back home at this time, for our protection.

Maria then rang me back and by the tone in her voice, was frustrated by our decision. I tried to make her understand the damage these allegations had caused and informed her that I had spoken to the family rights group and DC Romeria and based my decision on the information I received. As social services had taken her temporarily into care on the Monday, under the children's act, the decision lay with them about where to put her until support could be put in place for her to return home. She had not even spoken to DC Romeria about the outcome of the police investigation. Maria was adamant that Sophia had to be dropped back to me or they would take her round her aunt's house, but I stood my ground. I explained some of the problems we were having with Sophia, and she reckoned she had Asperger's syndrome, a form of autism. I did not understand how she came to this diagnosis, considering she was not employed as a mental health professional and had never met or spent any time with Sophia. Maria then said she would make a referral to Oak Avenue and that we would take it from there. I found out a week later when I rang her office that she had never faxed the referral form, as promised, to Oak Avenue, so her colleague ended up faxing it over. This was the start of many disastrous in competencies by Social Services, which impacted our lives greatly. I expressed my concerns about putting her with the Greens, but the decision was not in my hands; it was in theirs.

Later that day Maria rang back and told us Sophia's Aunt Pat would be picking her up from my friend Caroline's house tomorrow afternoon and told us we could go round and see Sophia before she went.

Sophia had been there for the last five days, ever since the allegations were made, and I had not seen or spoken to her since the Sunday evening when she came home from the party. By the time we arrived at my friend's house, we were tense and nervous. I don't know why I felt like this. It was not like I was meeting a stranger for the first time; this was my firstborn child, who I had nurtured and loved since the beginning of her life. My friend was running a few minutes late, so we stood outside in the fresh autumn air.

The fresh air was like a sedative, as I had not slept more than a few hours in five days. Now with the wind blowing in my face, I felt like I could sleep forever. Soon enough Caroline pulled up in her drive and greeted us with a supportive hug. Out of the corner of my eye, I saw Sophia climb out of the car almost as if she did not want us to see her come out. Ryan said hello to her, and she responded back, but I could not even look at her. I felt nervous to look at my own child, and a whole spectrum of emotions went through me in the few seconds, but I eventually looked at her.

We all went inside the house, and Ryan and I sat in the front room waiting for Caroline and Sophia to join us. Ryan and I whispered among ourselves thoughts on our initial contact with Sophia, wondering if she was sorry for the lies she had told, but it turned out to be far from the case. Sophia sat on a sofa to the side of us and my friend in the opposite chair across the room. I managed to say hello to her, and then Ryan asked her why she had made these accusations against him. Sophia did not respond. I became angry with her but kept my voice in a very measured tone and asked why she felt the need to lie about not wanting to see her dad; I told her we knew everything she had been doing, as the social worker had told us. Sophia tried to deny it, and by the look on her face, she was shocked we knew the depths of her deceit. Caroline asked her if she realised the seriousness of what she had done and asked her if she had anything to say to us, but there was no response.

Just by looking at her, I knew her heart had turned hard toward us and that she had made up her mind about the choices she made. I had never seen this side to her before. Usually at home, if she had been caught in a lie or if she knew she had done something wrong, she would say sorry after a while. She had beautiful, telling eyes that would give away the emotion she was feeling. But not this day; she was very different. No amount of asking her why or telling her the effect and devastation these accusations had on us, Esther, and Ryan's mum, who she had a close relationship with, had any effect. Ryan broke down and cried, but I could not cry. Ryan told her he loved her and that he forgave her for what she had done, but I could not even utter those words. I probably come across as a cold, unforgiving person, and many people would use this as another scenario to judge me, but until you have lived through this experience, no one has the right to tell me what I should have said or how I should have acted.

I told Sophia how I felt about her behaviour: that it was selfish and wicked and that I could not understand how she could use the fact that I was abused against us to get her own way when she had seen firsthand some of the challenges I still faced, seventeen years after the abuse had taken place. Sophia had told the social worker she did not wish to return home, and I told her at the time I did not want her back home, as I was disgusted with her behaviour. It was time for me to leave my friend's house before I said something bad, out of a place of hurt that I would regret later.

We left the house and had not driven far down the long road when my husband pulled over to the side of the road. He got out and went round and leaned on the boot of the car. At first I thought he needed to get something out of the boot, but after a few minutes, I got out to find him crying. I put my arm around his shoulder to comfort him, but I did not know what to say. He looked like how I felt—exhausted and sad. We did not know where we would start to pick up the pieces but hoped time would bring healing and clarity for the both of us. His phone rang, and it was his solicitor confirming what we had been told—that the police investigation was over and advised us that we could call her anytime if we needed help with anything else.

Two days later, on a Sunday evening, Sophia's Uncle Donald called to ask for the social worker's number. I asked him why he wanted her number, and he told me he just wanted to ask some questions. I keep the phone call very short with him and gave him the number.

Monday October 13, 2008, Maria La Rue rang and wanted to arrange a meeting for the following day with Ryan and me, Sophia, and her uncle and aunt. She told me she would call the next day to tell us what time my husband and I should come in. I was looking forward to meeting her so I could find out how far along she was in sorting out the referrals in regards to further help.

Our friends and church had been so supportive, and based on their advice, I decided to ring Sophia's uncle Donald to arrange a meeting for Ryan and me to go round to his house to speak to Sophia. I thought that over the weekend she would have had time to think about her actions and our talk and maybe be remorseful for what she had done. It took a lot of courage for me to ring Donald, as I knew he had played a part in helping Sophia undermine us as parents. (Sophia had told an aunt on Ryan's side of the family weeks earlier that they were present at one of her dad's functions and knew she was there without our permission. They apparently told Sophia they would adopt her when she was older because she was not happy at home.)

This information came to light on the first day of Sophia making the allegation. I asked him when it was possible for us to come round to talk and fully expected they would want to be present, but I was not prepared for what happened next. Donald told me that he would have to book me an appointment in his diary and that the meeting would take place at his office.

I was taken aback, as in the fifteen years I had known this man, I never had to book an appointment to go round his house. This man had been my confidante, a man I had looked up to as a father, who gave me away at my wedding. He was present at my second daughter's birth and performed her dedication and was a friend of my husband who he played pool and hung out with, playing FIFA football on the PlayStation with on many occasions. Now all of a sudden, we had to book an appointment to speak to him at an office I had never been to before. Immediately I sensed something was not right and told Ryan what had happened. Ryan rang to find out why he wanted to meet at his office. Donald gave my husband an explanation about having to see a client, which he never mentioned to me before; he would not even tell me if Sophia would be there. We knew he was playing a game and told him we would not be meeting at all. He was not prepared for that and tried to convince us that his reason was genuine, but I knew in my spirit it was not.

I waited all Tuesday morning for the social worker to ring about our meeting, and after two hours of waiting, I decided to call. To my surprise, I was informed by another social worker that Maria was actually in a meeting with Sophia's aunt and uncle that very moment and told she would pass on the message. When Maria finally rang, I asked her why she was meeting with Donald and Pat without me present, considering I had parental responsibility. She claimed she had not meant this Tuesday and that I was never meant to be present at this meeting because it was arranged by Donald. She kept going on about how great Donald and Pat where, how wonderful they were for taking Sophia in, and what great work he did in the community. (He ran a sports club at different schools.) Her response to me was to treat me like an emotional nutcase. Yet again, she could not grasp why I was extremely upset and distressed and commented that Donald said I would react like this. I told her that I had to go and that I would finish the conversation another time.

No sooner had I put down the receiver did Donald ring, sounding like someone who thought he had an upper hand. Triumphantly, Donald told me that they, meaning he and the social worker, had come to a decision that Sophia would be living with them from now until they decided when it was fit for her to return home. I told him this meeting should not have taken place without me being present, and he dismissively responded by telling me I was not invited. I later found out from an official document that they had told the social worker they believed Sophia had an unhappy childhood and that they could provide her with a stable and happy home until she was an adult.

The realisation of my naïveté suddenly hit me, and I knew he would use my times of vulnerability against me. I had confided in him during therapy sessions, and as he was talking to me, he tried to use his psychological experience against me. At one point in my life, I took everything Donald said as gospel and truth and never questioned whether what he said was right or wrong. He seemed like a good person who put other people's needs before his own, always acting like he measured any decisions he made by the Word of God. But I realised in that moment his number-one aim was to be in control at all the times and that he had his own agenda. He never made mistakes and never admitted at times, even when it was obvious, that he was wrong. Although he had known me well and had seen my struggles and victories in my personal life, I knew he was not going to speak the truth about me. That was the last time I ever spoke to Donald or his family.

I was trying my hardest to listen to people's advice about doing the right thing but struggled to keep my emotions in check, due to sheer frustration. I was trying to work with social services, but it was becoming apparent that they were not interested in what I had to say; it was like banging my head against a brick wall.

The conversation with Donald left me feeling vulnerable, so I rang the governing body for counsellors to find out if an ex-therapist could use information regarding your emotional state against you. The lady I spoke to told me it would be unethical for a counsellor to do this and suggested I request a complaints form for them to investigate. Only in extreme circumstances, if I was deemed at risk of endangering myself or others, could information relevant to the situation be requested by legal authorities. I also phoned the evangelical alliance, which is the largest church governing body in the U.K., to make a complaint about his conduct as a church minister, only to find the church he ran with his friend was not listed anywhere, under any umbrella of any church and was not listed as a small church either. I was angry and felt helpless. I knew it would be hard for me to prove his behaviour, as up to this point, there was no paper trail, and based on his outward character and position in the local community, I stood no chance.

Oak Avenue Centre eventually rang me on Monday October 20, 2008, ten days after initial referral was made. I spoke to them at length about some of the problems I was experiencing with Sophia, and they suggested that I come in to the centre with her. They were surprised when I informed them that Sophia was not living with me, as the social worker had not told them she was not living at the house. They explained that in order for the referral to proceed, they would need permission from Sophia for it to go ahead.

I was very frustrated at the lack of communication the social worker was providing and decided to make a formal complaint to Maria La Rue's supervisor at Social Services. Her supervisor seemed genuinely concerned about the case, and we arranged to meet on November 10, 2008. This situation with Maria La Rue had been going on four weeks, and not once had she wanted to meet with me to discuss my concerns, and even relaying information to other agencies was not done properly. Ryan and I were very frustrated and found dealing with social services just as stressful as dealing with the initial investigation into the allegations. I made sure I wrote down all the points that Ryan and I wanted to raise, as he would not be present, as he had just started a new job, and I also wrote down questions we wanted answers to. The morning of the meeting, her supervisor did not turn up, and half an hour later, I called her to find out where she was. She told me that she had an emergency court case and therefore, was unable to meet. We arranged another meeting for the next day and again she did not come round and did not call. That time when I spoke to her, I expressed my frustration and told her that I did not think she was taking the situation seriously.

The supervisor immediately went on to attack and accused me of being difficult. I was upset that we were not being heard, and because I wanted answers and challenged them, I was seen as being uncooperative. Again, another example of their communication came to light when she informed me that Donald and Pat had gone on holiday to Cyprus and left Sophia with their nineteen-year-old daughter Hazel, who Donald apparently said I gave permission to look after her while they were away. Apparently Maria La Rue said she was in the same room as Donald when he called me to ask. I asked the supervisor how she knew who Donald was on the phone to and how this qualified as asking me for direct permission. The supervisor informed me that the information was on Sophia's file, yet no one had verbally consulted me about any decision. The conversation ended badly, with the supervisor not taking any responsibility for not turning up to any of the meetings that were arranged. I wanted so badly to scream at this woman, but I realised that it would get me nowhere.

The next day I received a letter from Maria La Rue on behalf of social services, stating that they were looking to hold a case conference to decide whether my children were in need of child protection. Also in the letter she said that I gave permission for Sophia to stay with the Greens' nineteen-year-old daughter and that although the police investigation was closed, they would still be looking to investigate. I cannot explain to you how broken-hearted I was at seeing my family being destroyed. Far from the situation getting better, it was getting worse, and there was nothing I could do, apart from pray to Jesus. We were about to be hung, and he was our only hope.

I rang Maria La Rue and asked her in which conversation with her had I given permission for Sophia to stay with Donald and Pat's nineteen-year-old daughter. Her response was astonishing; she said she was in the room when Donald rang me and I gave permission and that the conversation was recorded. At that point I lost my temper and told her she was a liar and that I wanted to hear this taped conversation where I apparently gave permission. I informed her that I was going to make a complaint to the head of social services because she had not followed any procedures in any aspect of handling this case. I asked her why, after nearly five weeks since having this case, she had not arranged any meetings with me, only with Donald and Pat Green, who were not Sophia's legal guardians. She could not answer, and far from the defensive attitude she had previously displayed, her tone softened as she asked if she could come round and finally meet me that afternoon.

At first I said yes, as she said she could be at my house in half an hour, but when I rang my sister-in-law, Cheryl, to tell her about the latest incident with the social worker, she advised me that under no circumstance should I meet with her by myself. So I rang her back and told her she could not come round. Maria wanted to arrange another meeting with the Greens present, but I flatly refused. We wanted to meet with her on our own terms without the Greens being present, as she was already far too influenced by them in her decision making, so a separate meeting was set for us to see her two days later. She seemed eager to appease me, and I believe she knew she had not behaved with integrity in her handling of the case, and that was why she was now trying to cover her tracks. She knew she should have consulted me first regarding any aspects of Sophia's care.

By the time Ryan arrived home, I had drank two large wine glasses of vodka and orange juice and was looking to drink some more. As Ryan sat and read the letter, I sat contemplating taking my life. I could see no hope for us in this situation; the odds were stacked high against us with no end in sight. We were like invisible people the authorities could not see or hear, and I was tired of the tears and pain. I was in a desert—a place where the heat was constantly beating down on me. I was disoriented and exhausted and wanted an oasis of rest and replenishment, but in every direction I looked, all I could see were miles of dry land with no respite, no peace, and certainly no hope. Ryan went and picked up Esther from the child-minder's, and I turned up Tupac's song "Shed So Many Tears" on my stereo loud and drank another glass of vodka and orange juice as I stood in front of the large mirror in our front room with a carving knife pressed against my throat.

I looked at my face, and I could see the raw pain oozing out of me. I wondered how many buckets of tears I had cried over my whole life, and I was bitter about the hand I was given in life. I could feel the blade making a groove in my neck, and then the phone rang; it was a friend from church. I told her about the letter and what I was just about to do, and she came round with the pastor of our church. Ryan was upset to find out that again I was considering killing myself, and in that moment, when I thought about Esther and my husband, I knew that, even though I was in pain, they were suffering also. Suicide was not the answer, and I knew if I did it, I did not know for sure where my soul would end up. It was a desperate place to be in when I felt all hope has gone. Suicide felt like the only option, but there were no guarantees that when I physically died, my suffering would end. Time and time again, I was encouraged to put my hope in the one who could bring me out—God. I could not see how he could bring us out of this situation, but I had to learn to put my trust in him.

We went back to church for the first time in ages, and I was overcome with emotion. Ryan and I decided it would be good to go back, as we had not been in six weeks, and we were looking for God to comfort and reassure us through his Holy Spirit that he was with us. I sang with all my heart to God. I did not want to focus on our problems, but on him, even if it was only for a couple of hours. I knew God knew the truth, and I wanted him to make it known. People looked at me as I cried aloud, but I did not care. I was desperate for help.

Our friends prayed with us afterward, and as I was praying, I was reminded of Daniel 3:6, where God's prophets were thrown into the blazing furnace because they would not worship King Nebuchadnezzar's gold idol he had made. Shadrach, Meshach, and Abednego were thrown into the furnace and told King Nebuchadnezzar that they trusted God to deliver them out, but if it was not God's will they still would not worship his gold idol. God brought them out of that furnace not even smelling of smoke, despite the king turning it up to the highest heat. I felt God was telling Ryan and me that no matter what allegations were thrown at us, he would make sure that they would not stick against our names, that we would come out of this situation with our reputations intact because he was able to deliver us out, no matter how much heat and pressure rained down on us. We gained comfort from this, and I held on to it throughout the pain, which was constantly there.

We went to meet with Maria La Rue at her office. Her supervisor was meant to be present as well but, once again, had another emergency. We only agreed to meet with Maria because she said her supervisor was attending, so we felt she had tricked us. Immediately our backs went up, and we did not trust meeting with her one bit. Instead, in her supervisor's place, she brought a fellow colleague who was not a manager and not associated with the case. She asked me how I felt and said how difficult it must be to choose between my husband and daughter. I chose not to respond, as I knew full well she was capable of twisting information. We asked her a couple of questions, but she had no information to give us. To us this meeting was just as we thought—an attempt to tick the boxes she neglected to cover in the first place. Calmly, my husband told her that at this point in time Sophia could not come back home. They arranged to come and collect her stuff but, as usual, did not stick to the arrangement. On that note we left, not achieving any of the objectives we set, but I was now desensitised to the situation and expected nothing to be resolved through Social Services.

So it was left to my husband to drop Sophia's belongings round to Donald's house, and it was a hard situation to face. We knew what he had been saying to social services and the dangerous game he was playing, so again we had to pray and ask God to give Ryan the grace to deal with him without getting angry. My friend came round and helped me pack up my daughter's stuff, and it was sad packing it all into black bags. It drained all the strength I had left in me to do this as I looked at all the mementos of times we shared. Before it was loaded up into the car we prayed over her stuff and asked God to protect her. Then Ryan and his friend drove down to Donald's house.

I was on tenterhooks waiting for Ryan to come back and was hoping there were no altercations. When Ryan came back, he told me that Donald said he wanted to sort out the situation about Sophia between us because if social services found out about my past, meaning the fact I was abused and taken into care, it could go against me. He said they would look after Sophia now, as she had caused us enough trouble. His arrogance astounded me and the value he believed his influence on any situation would bring, like some sort of superhero that whatever he got involved in the outcome would always be good. Ryan was annoyed when he said this but did not show it, nor did he divulge any information to him, as he was probing for it. He simply unloaded the car and left.

December 8, 2008, the morning of the case conference, was tense and worrying, but we chose to do what we tried to do all along: pray. It was coming up to Christmas, but we had not done any Christmas shopping and were in no mood to celebrate. There was no time to get any presents with everything that had been going on, as it now had been just over two months since it all started. We were both very tired, and the stress affected our health badly in different ways. Ryan is a tall and slender man, who, if he misses a meal will lose weight; he had lost over half a stone because of the stress. I also lost weight but was more mentally troubled and paranoid because of the sudden events that had taken place in our lives. My sister-in-law came with us to the conference, and we were told to get there fifteen minutes before so we could speak to the chairwoman. We had received no paperwork and had not a clue what to expect, and it was only when we met with her that we saw any paperwork. Maria La Rue had gone back to Albania on compassionate leave, and another social worker, who we had never met, had taken over the case. No one knew why the case conference was called, and the whole meeting was a farce. Besides us, Cheryl, and the chairwoman was DC Romeria, the original child protection officer, the deputy head of Sophia's school, a health visitor, the new social worker, and his supervisor, whom we had never met or heard from before.

They had no information on us, as the new social worker had never met us, and he informed us in the meeting that he was also leaving at the end of the week. There was conflicting and missing information in the report written by social services, and we then got to find out for the first time the different version of events Sophia gave to her class teacher, deputy head, and the police. The chairwoman was dismayed and shocked at the lack of efficiency in preparing for the case conference and had no choice but to adjourn it. She told the social workers that they needed to meet with us, Sophia's dad, Sophia, Donald, and Pat individually to discuss everyone's view. I was in some part relieved to hear this, as they had only been interested in Donald and Pat's point of view up until now. I had to have a visit from the health visitor at the conference so she could observe how Esther interacted with me in the home environment so she could compile a report. They were many other surprises that came out of the meeting, but I cannot go into many details about this. As the conversation continued between the different agencies, I glanced through the report that had been written and found it upsetting to see some of the comments people I once trusted had made. We decided, with my sister-in-law's help, to write a letter to our local Member of Parliament to make a complaint about our treatment and also write a formal letter to the head of social services and complaints department and request a copy of any files containing information about our family. We were disappointed that we would have to go through another case conference but accepted that this was part of the process.

Ryan and I feared hearing the letterbox clank, as we had developed a psychological fear to seeing brown envelopes on the doormat because they always contained bad news from social services. On the doormat was a brown envelope; it contained a letter from Mayday Hospital open day surgery unit to our doctor at our doctor's surgery regarding Sophia's foot operation. The letter said that due to the new information that had come to light, they were willing to reinstate her on the list for the operation. I rang Mayday to find out about this new information and was greeted by the surgeon's secretary, who frostily told me to contact my GP, as she refused to give me any information. I rang the doctor's surgery and asked the receptionist what information was given by the doctor. She told me that Donald and Pat came to the surgery with my daughter Sophia and told the doctor that there was a court protective order out against me because I had abused my daughter and that any decision regarding her health was to be referred to them. I demanded to speak to the manager and asked her what evidence the doctor saw to state there was a court order against me. She said they gave none and that the information given was taken on their word. I was livid and asked her how someone can just walk in off the street and make these allegations that have been put on an official document without proof. She could not answer my question but made an appointment for me to see one of the GP practice partners.

When I eventually saw the GP, he told me that he had spoken to the doctor involved, and she confirmed the conversation with the Greens took place. He could not answer why this was allowed to happen but gave his word that he would investigate. Distressed, I told him at no point had there ever been an order against me, and I gave him the name of the social worker to contact to confirm this. It was as though I forever had to prove my innocence while people like Donald and Pat Green could go round saying and doing what they liked. Bitterness started to take root in my soul, and I spent many a time rehearsing evil thoughts in my mind towards them. Sometimes I delighted in this but knew it would only lead to destruction, so I asked God to forgive and help me rise above my emotions. I was angry, but I am not a malicious and vindictive person.

I asked the GP to remove the information from her file, as it was not true, but he told me that under the law, I would have to get Sophia's consent to remove it, which I knew she would not give. Although they needed her permission, I had to give them permission in writing to write to her to get that consent. I believed the doctor when he said he would investigate, and he wrote a letter to the Greens, which he sent me a copy of, asking them to produce proof of this court order. The heat just kept being piled on, and I left his office in tears. He rang a few days later and informed me that neither my daughter nor the Greens responded to the requests and that he would continue to try to get the matter resolved. He had left a couple of messages for the new social worker that was on the Sophia's case to clarify there was no court order but was waiting for him to return his calls. It was unjust and unfair that people could just walk into an official establishment such as a doctor's surgery and slander my name.

Our hands were tied, and the Greens seemed to control the situation wherever they went. It was apparent to me that all authorities took their word as bond because of his position as a church minister and his family's place in the local community, which they used to their advantage, while my word was worthless. I was so incensed and outraged that I called solicitors in between preparing for the second case conference, Christmas, and drafting notes for my sister-in-law. I had a case for slander, as they were not just making false statements; they were leaving a paper trail in the form of the discussion with the doctor that was on their computer records. Filing a slander case was expensive—three hundred pounds an hour—and that was before any real action had begun, so in the end it would cost us around ten thousand pounds. Ryan and I considered taking out a loan, as we were so angry, but this was not what God wanted us to do. I was not thinking about the long-term prospect of paying back the debt, as I was reacting in anger. We ended up not taking out the loan and succumbed to the fact that our hands were tied.

That situation had not even passed when the next day another brown envelope landed on our doormat on a Saturday morning. Brown envelopes never came on a Saturday, always on a weekday. Weekends we felt we could breathe a little and get some peace, but what happened next shattered that safe haven Saturday always brought for us.

The letter was from Maria La Rue on behalf of her supervisor, stating that new evidence had come to light regarding statements from people who witnessed inappropriate behaviour displayed by Ryan and me and that I was to present my two-year-old daughter, Esther, to social services first thing on Monday morning the 24th of November. Ryan and I sat stunned and trying to rack our brains as to who would say they witnessed inappropriate behaviour from us. We did not mix with anyone in Croydon apart from a few close friends at our church, as our other friends we mixed with lived in Battersea. We knew it was to do with the Greens but could not pinpoint who in the family it was. The weekend was ruined for us, and we spent the whole of it anxious and afraid that Esther was going to be taken away from us.

Cheryl drove down from Ilford to come to the meeting with social services on Monday morning. She had managed to find out from her friend who was high up in another borough's social services that this meeting was basically a knee-jerk reaction to events, as they should have seen Esther when the original allegations happened eight weeks before. They were basically covering the bases they should have have covered from the beginning, but it did nothing to reassure us; it just felt like a continuation of bad events.

Just before I left, I rang to inform the supervisor that my sister-in-law was running ten minutes late. I asked her why I had to bring Esther, but she said they had never met her and would like to see her. The letter did not give the tone of a cheery visit like how she tried to come across on the phone.

We arrived at social services office and informed the receptionist we were there to see Maria La Rue and her supervisor. When the receptionist rang the supervisor, she informed her that an emergency case had come up and she would not be attending the meeting she had called, and we also found out that Maria La Rue had left her job a few days before the letter was sent out in her name. Cheryl asked the receptionist to put the supervisor on the phone, but the supervisor refused to take our call. I had just spoken to her from my home not even half an hour before and she confirmed that she was attending. Again, they treated us with no respect, and their contempt for us was making me sick.

They were not thinking of the distress receiving a letter demanding I present Esther to them would cause. I had taken her out of going to her childminder's for the day to attend their meeting at a whim. Cheryl and I were disgusted. The supervisor then sent down one of her staff to meet with us, but from talking to her, she knew nothing about the case and admitted she was given this file only ten minutes before. I kept my mouth closed, as I was at the exploding point and knew I would end up saying something very bad. Cheryl asked her why a letter was sent out in Maria La Rue's name when she had left the employment of social services a few days before. We could even see on the letter that the date had been tippexed out and a new date inserted on top. She could not answer why I had to bring down Esther or what the "new evidence" that had come to light was. All she told us was that a man came into the office and handed an envelope containing four statements to the receptionist. She never asked me about Esther and did not acknowledge her presence once. This was a pointless time-wasting exercise that showed their consistent incompetence. Cheryl took her name and noted the conversation; then we left.

Far from accepting what had just happened, as soon as we got back home, we phoned the supervisor at her office. Tellingly, the emergency she had twenty minutes ago had now passed, and she was now willing to speak to me on the phone. She told me the four people who sent in these statements about inappropriate behaviour were Sophia, her dad, and her two female cousins Hazel and Ingrid—Donald and Pat's teenage daughters. The statements were apparently forwarded to the police a week before, and I was very worried about what these statements would mean for us. Stress caused some of my hair to fall out, and I really could not take any more nasty surprises, so I rang DC Romeria to find out if she had received any statements, as the supervisor said they had been sent to the child protection unit. DC

Romeria said they received no statements, and she even searched the police database to see if any were sent in by social services, but there were none. She said social services should know better than anyone how malicious people's families could be, especially as the original case was closed with the police over six weeks ago and none of these family members made any allegations then. Social services had not spoken to any of these family members to investigate further the information that was sent to them. They just said they sent them to the police.

The man who handed the statements in was Sophia's dad, and funnily enough I thought it was Donald. I can't say I was surprised to find out it was him, as this was fitting of his character, but I was intrigued to find out what new accusations my daughter had made. For the life of me, I could not figure out what story Donald's daughters made up but knew they were full of dramatics, so I knew it would be bad.

The very situation I feared and warned social services about had now come to pass, escalating into a huge drama, just as I said would happen. Their hatred of us was very clear, and they wanted their own form of justice. I could not figure out how these people who had nothing to do with the situation from the start were now central to everything that was going on. How Sophia's dad felt toward us was always glaringly obvious, but the Greens never showed any of these hateful signs towards us before. Only four months before, Donald and Pat's nineteen-year-old daughter, Hazel, had invited Ryan and me to her wedding. Ryan had even stopped her wedding reception from being a disaster when the DJ she hired pulled out. At the time my husband was a manager of an electrical store, so Donald asked him for loan of music equipment, which my husband was happy to provide. Ingrid, their youngest, who was close in age to Sophia, stayed over at our house often, and the eldest daughter Hazel and Pat were both godmothers to Esther. So you can see by our relationship with them, this hardly was the behaviour of people who hated us.

It was now the week of Christmas, and we had not bought any cards or presents for anyone, so hurriedly I went down to Croydon

Shopping Centre to pick up a few last-minute bits. On my travels I saw at least three of Sophia's dad's relatives, and I avoided eye contact with them, but I did not know why I did this; I had done nothing to be ashamed of, yet I was walking around like I had. I did not look anyone in the eye anymore, apart from those who loved us, as people outside of our network had already cast their judgement about us. I desperately wanted to leave Croydon and could not wait for the house exchange to go through.

I walked around for ages, paranoid I would bump into anyone else I knew. My heart pounded in my chest so hard I thought I would pass out. Even before all this had happened, I only went into Croydon first thing in the morning, as I hated crowds, so imagine what it felt like going into Croydon two days before Christmas in the evening. At first I refused to think about buying Sophia any Christmas presents, but after much soul searching, Ryan and I decided to go against our own selfish feelings and do what we considered God would want us to do. After all, Jesus came and died for us even though we did nothing to deserve forgiveness. Actions speak louder than words, so if I proclaimed to be a Christian, I must also operate out of that same love. Sophia did not deserve a present because of her behaviour, but we would buy her one because she was our daughter and we loved her, and that is how God is with us. We bought her a pair of low-ankle boots and pair of trainers that I knew she liked. A friend from church had offered to come and collect the presents on Christmas Eve and drop them to her at her family's house. It was too late to arrange to have them dropped to her school, as they had already broken up for the holidays. DC Romeria had advised us after the first conference that if we were going to send her any presents or cards, we should send them to the school. I hope she received her presents, as my friend handed them to Donald when he opened his door on Christmas Eve.

My first Christmas without Sophia was hard emotionally, as my mood swung between tearful and jokey throughout the day. For nearly the last two and a half months, this whole affair had consumed so much of our life that I had not spent much time focusing on Esther. There was only so much moping around I could do, and as the saying goes, life goes on, the world keeps turning and morning still turns to night. Life was not going to stop, but my life as I knew it certainly had, and that was scary.

In the spurts of the day feeling normal, Ryan and I made sure Esther had a good Christmas. Ryan and I always went round to his mum's house at Christmas and usually drove down on Christmas Eve, but as we had spent so much time down there over the last couple of months, we decided to go Christmas morning. Esther noticed Sophia was not there with us, and only a month after it all happened, she had started asking where Sophia was. It was hard to try to explain, so we told her in a way she could understand—that Sophia was at her friend's house. For that first month when I dropped Sophia to the childminder's, she would not let go of my leg and became extremely clingy, which she had never been before. I cannot imagine how her little mind could begin to grasp that one minute her sister and she were together and now her sister had disappeared. Circumstances were out of our control, and while it was hard for her, Ryan's family, Esther's minder, and church supported us in dealing with this aspect. I know it is no consolation, but we made sure that she and her cousin Natalie, who is one year older than her, spent as much time as possible, and it helped.

Esther spent most of her time running round with her cousin as soon as we stepped in the house. There were plenty of people round that day so we were in good company and did not have much time to think about the upcoming conference. I thought about how Sophia's Christmas was going and was sure it was going well, as she had her dad and more importantly her freedom. Certainly from what the Greens relayed to social services in the previous case conference report, this seemed to be the case. I hoped for her sake all the pain these lies caused was worth it.

In the Midst of Fire

The Christmas period was over, and along came the start of many different meetings and visits I had to endure with a whole range of people. The first was a visit from the health visitor who was at the case conference. I could tell from when she walked in the door scanning around my living room with her eyes that this was going to be a tough visit. I was nervous the night before, and when morning came, I made sure the house was tidy. I was tense and on edge, but I thought I answered all of her questions adequately. Admittedly, I never offered her a drink, as this was not a social visit and I resented the fact I was under scrutiny, but I was polite and spoke when spoken to. She was annoyed when I told her that I did not have Sophia's red health book and asked where it was. I told her I could not remember, as I had not had that book since Sophia was small, so that was strike one against my name. She observed Esther painting a picture and interacting with me and was happy with that, and then she wanted to talk about how I was coping, as she knew I had a history of depression. I was happy to talk her about Esther's and Sophia's health, but I was not comfortable talking to her about my feelings or about my feelings towards Sophia. I told her it was not appropriate for us to mention Sophia in front of Esther and that I did not want to discuss how I felt. I knew what she was here to do—to compile a report for the social services conference—and I did not trust her. I was trying, in part, to keep things normal for Esther and did not want her to get upset at the mention of her sister's name, as she had only recently start to accept that she was at a friend's house. So this, coupled together with the health book and lack of refreshments, were my three strikes, and she was not about to forget it. She was only at my house for about forty minutes, but it felt like she was there all day; I was relieved when she left.

My sister-in-law arranged for me to meet the MP to voice our dissatisfaction with the handling of our case. My friend Caroline, who looked after Sophia that first week, met me at the MP's office in Thornton Heath. I got there early, as I did not want to be late, and sat in the waiting room looking over the complaint letter to help refresh my memory. I was mentally tired and was not confident that I would be able to articulate my point effectively. I had no confidence in any of the agencies I had met so far and had repeated myself so many times with little effect. None of them could see why we found it so upsetting. Maybe they had become desensitised because they dealt with these scenarios so often. Cheryl really had to coax me into going because of this very reason, and at first I was not sure it was a good idea. But I was not the only one in this situation that was upset, and as I was the only person who had the legal right to complain, I pushed past my negative attitude and used this as motivation to go.

The MP asked me to explain very quickly the situation and what I wanted him to do, as he had other people waiting. The time allocated to me was only about fifteen minutes, and pressure to deliver in such a short time led to me getting confused about some of the timeline of events. His assistant made notes of points to cover in the letter that would be sent to the director of social services, and my friend filled in the gaps as I was speaking.

I am grateful she took time to come straight from teaching at her school to come and support me, but I left feeling the meeting did not go well, despite her assurances it did. The meeting came hastily to an end, with him promising to forward a copy of the letter he would send. I think because the MP kept looking at his watch and hurrying me along when I spoke, this might have contributed to me feeling the meeting was a failure. Caroline drove me home, and I cried my eyes out. I was tired and wanted it all to end.

Cyril was the third social worker assigned to our case and the first one we actually sat down with to have a proper meeting on December 31, 2008. He had come round to talk to me and find out what issues we wanted to address and told me what I should expect in the second case conference. He was putting together a report to present at the conference and was meeting with everyone who was involved. He had already met with the Greens on two occasions when he went round to see Sophia but told me that he was not able to speak to her on her own, as they were constantly present. But from what he said, she was apparently happy to live there. Cyril was unaware of the meetings that took place without me present and was surprised when I told him the nature of my previous relationship with the Greens, as they had not told him. I mentioned the slanderous accusations they made to the doctor at the surgery about the court order, and he was puzzled as to where they got this information from. He asked me what Sophia's dad was like, and I told him he would see for himself. He was asking this because Sophia had originally wanted to live her dad and wanted to know if this was a possible option. He was meeting with her dad the following afternoon so he could get his view as well. I was not concerned about what Sophia's dad had to say, because I expected he would blame me as usual. My main concern was to get mine and Ryan's view across, and he listened to what I had to say and seemed to value the points I made. As he was leaving, he said maybe Sophia's main motivation to stay round the Greens was because she had her cousin Ingrid, who was a similar age, to relate to. He could understand why things were the way they were and asked me, although I could not be reconciled with her at the moment, not to close the door and give up on her for good. I had never given up on her for good but was so far removed from her in my emotions because we were still having to fight to clear our names of wrongdoing. Reconciling was not the first thing on my mind, and anyway, this was not about just me; it was about Ryan and Esther too.

We arrived at the office for the case conference on January 8, 2009 late, so immediately I took this as a sign things were not going to go well. We were supposed to receive the case conference report days before the meeting, but as usual, due to lack of efficiency, ended up being handed the report fifteen minutes before.

When the Greens walked in, I did not acknowledge them at all, but my husband said hello as they passed. It was an awkward situation, but I handled it better than I thought I would. I knew the Greens were attending, as Cyril had told me in advance they were invited, but he did not tell me that Sophia's dad was coming. When he walked into the waiting area, I was not scared or intimidated, just calm. I did not even look at him. He sat away a few chairs away from his aunt and uncle, which the chairwoman noticed and stopped talking mid-flow, commenting on the body language between them. She said from what the Greens had conveyed in the report, they were a close family. She was also annoyed because from reading the report, she said this should never have been a child protection conference but a child-in-need support meeting, as all the agencies that made their reports—Sophia's school, the new social worker, and police—believed my children were not in any danger. Hearing her say this was slightly reassuring, but I was still paranoid that there would be more nasty surprises in store, and only when I heard the official outcome of the conference would I feel able to breathe. Cyril had asked Sophia, her dad, and Donald and Pat's daughter's for consent for me to read their statements, but all of them said no. I did not understand why they would not let us see them. They were happy sneaking around, plotting our downfall, making accusations behind our backs but not brave enough to bring it out in the open, so we were still in the dark.

The chairwoman was a black lady in her forties, and I found her a bit imposing in stature, as she had quite a serious demeanour. Before we went in to the meeting, she went through the report with us and told me I should never have said during the interview with the police and social worker that I would not have Sophia back home if the allegations were true or untrue, because it looked like I had my perfect little family now, in which Sophia was not included.

I tried to explain to her that the comment was taken out of context in a situation I found extremely distressing. But I had given up on anyone believing anything I had to say, and now my attitude was one of "think what you want." Because I accepted that people would think what they wanted about me, it gave me a slight release in my people-pleasing ways. Most of my life I had spent trying to please people and worrying what they said about me and gained nothing from it, apart from disappointment. God knew my heart, and only God could judge me if I had done wrong in dealing with this situation. And if this was the case, then this conference would be my downfall. I told her I was not happy about Sophia's dad attending the meeting and explained to her he was physically and emotionally abusive to me in the past and that he continued to be verbally threatening towards my husband when he could not have his way when arranging visits for Sophia. She gave her word that she would be fully in control of the conference and that if he displayed any such threatening behaviour, he would have to leave.

The meeting was twice the size of the last one because of the additional people that were invited. Besides myself, my husband, Cheryl, and Ellen, my friend from church, there was Sophia's dad, Donald and Pat Green, Cyril, the social worker and his supervisor, the deputy head of Sophia's school, the health visitor, the chairwoman, and the minute taker. DC Romeria could not attend but had someone read her report on her behalf. We all sat around a huge table and had to introduce ourselves. This was the first time I actually looked at Sophia's dad properly and was not the only person in the room who was shocked by his appearance. Everyone was looking at him. He had unusually dark rings under his eyes. He looked like life had not been kind to him over the years, and far from making an effort to dress appropriately for such a meeting, he wore a tracksuit top and bottom that did not match, which added to him looking very dishevelled.

Again, I cannot go into much detail about what happened at the conference, but God was definitely on our side. Donald and Sophia's dad's arrogance and maliciousness got exposed for what it was, because when it came down to the crunch, they tried to bring us down with a pack of lies. My husband mentioned the information the Greens gave the doctors, and it so happened that the deputy head said Donald and Pat had done the same at Sophia's school. They had the school secretary put on Sophia's file that there was an order against me and that they should remove my contact details, but when the deputy head was preparing information for the conference, he spotted it. Sophia's dad was asked about the allegation he made of mistreatment by me. He said it had been going on a year, but when the chairwoman asked him why, if his daughter had come to him in continuing distress threatening to run away, did he wait a whole year to say something to anyone, he tried to say he did not know who to go to, but his motives were as clear as day. Then he threatened to kill my husband in front everyone. The chairwoman had the minute taker note this, but as I said, this behaviour was typical for him. I reported this incident to the police.

I got a hard time about everything from Sophia's health, (apparently her teeth were bad and other issues) to the friends she chose to make at our church. The chairwoman took this as I gave her no freedom to pick her own friends. I was under intense scrutiny and felt vulnerable and alone, as Ryan could not say much, as he was not a legal guardian. Apparently three weeks after the statements came to light, DC Romeria forwarded in her report for the conference they were faxed the previous morning to her. She stated there was nothing in them that could be considered new evidence, as most aspects were covered in initial interview with Sophia. This was good news for us, and I was glad we would not have to endure another police investigation.

There was only one professional person in the case conference who voted that Sophia was at possible risk if she returned home—the health visitor. She gave her reason, as when she came and visited me, I would not talk to her about Sophia, that I was tense at the mention of her name, and that I asked her not to talk about Sophia in front of Esther. I was not bothered by her decision and did not expect a favourable report from her but was pleased everyone else said that neither Sophia nor Esther were at harm in my home or anywhere else we would be with them. It was a victory, but a hollow one, and certainly not an occasion to break open champagne. It was a hard, hard experience I would not forget in a hurry. Social services wanted to arrange a mediation meeting between Sophia's dad and me to discuss Sophia, but both of us had to agree to it. I knew I would never subject myself to be in the same room with him ever again, as I had left that stress behind a long time ago. I was no longer the insecure Yvonne who put up with the ranting and verbal abuse. I was strong enough now not to put myself in that situation. They asked him first, and in doing that, they freed me of ever having to give my answer. He adamantly said there was no way it would ever happen, and for once we finally agreed on something.

It was only me, the chairwoman, Cyril, his supervisor, my husband, Cheryl, and Ellen left in the room when the chairwoman said to me that Donald was too involved in my life. Then Cyril said he was not impressed with their behaviour, especially Donald's, as he gave the impression he was a mediator in the situation but took his nephew's side. I reflected on this for a moment and said that blood was always thicker than water and that I had learned the hard way.

Who was I to think that Donald and Pat could love me like blood family? I was stupid to believe they could love me naturally like their own daughters. Sometimes, as was certain in my case, the love I thought they felt for me was used for control. Looking back, I can see that when I was weak, needy, and lonely, they were happy to pick up the pieces when I made a mess of things. Then it changed when I started to get on my feet, especially when I pulled away to make my own life with my husband. I learned a valuable lesson that day, and it was to never give away control of myself to anyone. I allowed myself to be controlled because I wanted to be loved and accepted. I had no one to guide me growing up who could help me put those boundaries in place. It was evident to these strangers I shared a room with for two hours the hold I gave them over my life, but I had not seen it in the fifteen years I knew the Greens.

I could not speak on the drive home and was very upset about what I read in the conference report, so as soon as my sister-in-law dropped us back, I grabbed my car keys and drove to Caroline's house. She held me as I cried and cried; I had never been so betrayed.

It had been a week since the conference, and I was due to return to work after being off sick for the last six months. I did not feel ready to go back, but after talking with Malcolm, who I had just started cognitive counselling with, I decided it might be what I needed to take my mind off my problems. I was still depressed about everything and felt humiliated by the experience. Thoughts of hate toward the Greens and Sophia's betrayal flooded my mind constantly, and I was holding on to the hurt and anger inside. No matter how many of my Christian friends advised me to forgive them, I could not.

There is a saying that goes "What is done in the dark will come out in the light," and that certainly applied when a week after the conference, the statements that Sophia, her dad, and her cousins tried to stop me reading landed on my doorstep one Saturday morning. They were attached to a court order filed by her dad against me for abuse and neglect and parental responsibility for himself. He was also seeking an order for Donald and Pat to be made Sophia's legal guardians, and I would have to attend a court hearing on February 18, 2009. I was upset at having to go through another legal process, but what was completely devastating was reading what my own daughter had said about me in her statement. She said I was a lazy and bad mother who slept all day and that she was the main carer for her sister, as she cooked all her meals and looked after her. She also said that she was stopped from seeing her family, especially her dad, and that I said the child he had with his girlfriend was not her sister and she was not to call her "sister." I had never said this to her, and I remember when her sister on her dad's side had her first Christmas. I actually took Sophia to Boots to buy her a present. Why would I take my money and do this if I did not want her to acknowledge her sister? I could not believe how this child could twist everything to make it sound worse than what it was.

There was an incident where both of my daughters were sick and my husband was leaving work to come home to sit with Esther, so in the meantime I called Sophia a cab to go to the doctor. The nurse called and told me that as she was under sixteen, I would have to be present, so when my husband returned, I went to the doctor to pick her up and then took her to Mayday Hospital, as she had a vomiting virus. What she said was that I only wanted to stay at home with Esther and showed no interest in her health at all. I did not have any family apart from my husband and tried to do my best in the situation. The nurse fully understood and kept her there until I arrived, as she knew Esther was too sick for me to take her out.

All the other stuff was about her not being allowed to see her dad and family. Ryan and I apparently banned her from them seeing them, telling her that they did not love her. When Sophia was living with us, especially during the nine months we decided to concentrate on our family, they rarely rang for her. Sophia was particularly upset, as the last time she saw her nan at her cousin's engagement in January 2008, their relationship was fine, but her nan did not call her again until July 2008 when she wanted to take her to a family get-together.

Ryan pointed out to her nan that it was upsetting for Sophia and that it was as though she was only wheeled out for their family occasions. Her nan was not pleased that he mentioned this, and when

I rang her back to ask her why she had no contact for six months, she did not return my call. Sophia had not one good thing to say about me in all the fourteen years. I brought her up to the best of my capabilities, yet her dad, according to her, had been a great dad who supplied all her needs. It was the same with her aunt and uncle and cousin Ingrid, who claimed to have an undying love for Sophia but yet had not called her once.

Sophia did not want to speak to them, so for all of them, this situation worked out conveniently, as they could blame us instead of taking responsibility themselves. In the papers filed, Jason also claimed that Sophia had lived with Donald and Pat most of her life and that he would like her to live there. How was Sophia going over for sleepovers on weekends and half term living there? The Greens had said the same in their report to the conference, but this was not true. They had always wanted Sophia to live with them, and when Ryan and I, a year earlier, experienced some normal teenage problems with her, the first thing they offered was for her to live there, but we said no. Sophia's dad claimed I was mentally unstable and that I stopped him from having a loving relationship with her. This would have been laughable if in a different situation, and I almost thought I had been sleeping for the last fourteen years. Was this the same dad who had left her standing at school gates on more than one occasion, who could not bother to take an interest in her apart from when it suited him? The truth was that he chose not have a consistent relationship with her yet made no mention of his own lacklustre and irresponsible attitude in his statement. What was so telling was he filed court papers for his aunt and uncle to become her legal guardians, yet he yearned all of his life to have a good relationship with her. I did not find his statement at all upsetting, as I had heard these same types of accusations on a worse scale during the years I had contact with him. I was only amazed at his audacity to file papers against me.

Hazel and Ingrid's statements were ridiculous, and no wonder DC Romeria said they were nothing to worry about, as they sounded like a good piece of storytelling. Hazel apparently witnessed a year before, conveniently when I was not in my house, an incident where my husband had brushed pasted Sophia's bum in the kitchen when she bent down. This had made her decide not ever to come to my house again, yet I have dated pictures of her in my house after this time, at Esther's first birthday and my thirty-first birthday party. If social services had bothered to investigate properly instead of just listening to the Green family's point of view, they would have known this and our workplaces would have confirmed we were not off the day before our daughter's first birthday, as they keep holiday records.

Ingrid, the youngest daughter, alleged that Sophia was never allowed to touch any of our electrical goods such as the stereo or computer and that whenever she saw Sophia, she was always so sad but now was happy again because she was living with them. These were the statements that social services were going to use to decide whether my children were at risk and were the basis of their whole investigation.

I was angry about having to go to court, but as was pointed out to me, it was merely a formality and the real end to nearly five months of pain. I went to see a solicitor who advised me on answering the questions in the petition. One of the questions asked was if I thought Sophia was at risk of harm from the claimant. I answered yes. I attached the copy of her schoolwork in which she gave details of verbal and physical harm she had experienced at his hands and details of the physical abuse I went through at his hands. I did not want to go through this again, as I had put it in my past, but I had no choice but to go through. I had to clear my name.

The day of the actual hearing, I could not eat and was very worried, even though I knew social services had made their decision and that the court would not file against it. I was worried because the day before when I went to give in my papers to the court, I arrived late. I was on a platform in Balham when a man threw himself under the train, which was not a pretty sight, and left me in great distress. I had left work early, but because of this incident I ended up reaching the court after four o'clock, when the office was closed. I ended up begging the security guard to hand them in and was not sure if the papers were handed in to the right department. Ryan and a couple of friends from church came with us for support, and we sat in the waiting room, waiting to be called. Donald and Pat walked in, closely followed by Sophia's dad. We sat on different sides of the room.

The case was called on time, and much to my horror, I had to go in by myself with Jason. The judge sat behind a huge desk reading the paper that was filed, and I could see he had my response, which I was worried had not reached them. We sat in silence for what seemed like an eternity, and inside I was shaking. I started to pray and ask God to protect and calm me through his Holy Spirit; this helped me. The judge asked me a series of questions, which I tried to answer, but Jason kept interrupting. He really wanted me to pay for whatever he felt I had done, and I could feel the attack pouring from his spirit; oppression filtered over the room. I kept my cool, and I could see the judge was listening to what I had to say. He asked if I said that I did not want contact with Sophia. I said yes.

He then asked if I now wanted phone contact, and I said if she wanted to contact me then that was okay. Jason interrupted again and informed the judge about the same comment I made during the police interview. This comment became the stick that the authorities and Sophia's family used to beat me over my head over and over again, no matter what I had said since; it was irrelevant. I asked the judge to imagine a child, who he had brought up since birth, making these accusations against him. I asked how he would feel in my shoes. Sophia had left us devastated, and that was why I responded the way I had.

Jason commented that if I wanted to call Sophia, I was to call Donald and Pat's house phone. He even commented that Donald gave me away at my wedding, trying to make them sound like the epitome of all that was good and right. I told the judge there was no way I would ever want anything to do with these people again, let alone call their home. I told the judge they had a huge part to play in the situation. I told the judge that reading what Sophia had said about me was devastating. Jason mentioned the bad health report made by the health visitor and referred to her conclusion in the second case conference report. I did not have mine at the time, as I had to send it back, as it was full of inaccuracies. The judge said there was something about Sophia having bad health, but I do not remember it saying I had clearly caused this.

In the end the judge asked if I objected to Jason having parental responsibility. I said no, so that was granted. In regards to the legal guardianship for his aunt and uncle, the judge said no and that they had to file for it themselves. He also said that as social services had already investigated the claims of physical and emotional abuse and found Sophia was not as risk, he was satisfied with their findings and would not be ruling otherwise. He said Sophia was now fifteen years old and would soon be at a legal age to make her own decisions, so in terms of contact, she could not be forced.

On leaving the courtroom, I was greeted by my husband and friends, and I broke down crying. I was glad the court had not forced me to have contact with Jason, and on him having parental responsibility, that meant he would now have to become the main parent who made all the decisions for her and support her financially.

Hope and a New Future

I am so thankful to God, who, yet again, delivered us out of the mouth of Satan, who waged a war through the Greens and Jason against Ryan and me for so long. For all their efforts, their victories were hollow, as nothing they planned to use to destroy us came to pass. Our children were not put on a child protection register; my husband was never interviewed, arrested, or charged; and I was not found by any judge or authority to be a bad or unfit mother. God was true to his word, just like he showed me in the story of Daniel when the three men were thrown into the furnace. God not only brought us out of the furnace; he also brought us out not smelling of the smoke of having our names or reputations tarnished and us as a family destroyed. Our friends and family were right—this was just an end to a long battle. Satan tried again to roar but was like a lion without any teeth; the sting was taken away from this situation because social services declared we were never a risk. God never sees the righteous forsaken.

We never received any worldly justice in the circumstances that we went through. The complaint that Ryan's sister wrote on our behalf never reached the person or department it was meant for. I rang to chase it up and found out it had not even been read and was sitting at the bottom of someone's office drawer. Hastily, they sent out a response to the complaint two days later after having it two months, which basically said that I should concentrate on keeping my kids safe from my husband. Again, if they had bothered to search their own files, they would have seen the outcome of the whole case. The GP eventually got confirmation from social services that there was no court order ever issued against me for abuse. He wrote me a letter to apologise and inform me that the information had now been removed from Sophia's medical file.

The aftermath for us as a family has been very damaging and affected mine and Ryan's marriage deeply. It became a barrier between Ryan and me for a long time and nearly drove us apart as we dealt with it in our own way instead of coming together.

Esther talks about her sister often, and we encourage her to. Sophia was an important part of her life for so long, and we do not want her to forget that. For many months I could not mention Sophia's name, let alone talk about her, because I was so angry. But through time I have learned to forgive her for what she has done, and in doing that, it has released me from anger and allowed me to start to heal. The pain will always be there, and I believe strongly that it is only going to be through God that our relationship, not just as mother and daughter, but as a family unit be restored.

In the Bible (Luke 15:11–32) is the story of a son who decides to go out from under his father's covering into the world to experience life on his own. He spends off his inheritance on wild living, and when the money runs out, he ends up in a situation where he is destitute. It is only then he comes to a place where he realises what he has done wrong and goes back to apologize to his father, who, instead of chastening him, welcomes him back with open arms.

This parable has given me hope for my Sophia, because it shows that while the son has done wrong, he eventually goes back and says sorry, and his father's response is one of love and forgiveness. At this point in my life, I am still estranged from my daughter, and I believe that Sophia has to admit to what she has done as part of the reconciling process. It will be a brave and honest admission for her to admit she lied. This is no easy feat because many people will probably be disappointed in her.

I always tried to teach her about consequences and responsibility of the choices we make, and the consequences for her have been severe. I believe she never meant for the situation to escalate the way it did and probably thought she could control the outcome. For Sophia, I know that she is also searching for a piece of her that she feels is missing, and looking back, I can see that no matter how much love we showed her or how we tried to include her in everything we did as a family, she did not feel part of it. A big part of her wanted that complete love from her dad, and that I can understand.

I could have run back and let her dictate to me the boundaries of our relationship and not held her accountable for her actions, and at times it has been hard to hold on to what I believed was right because I have missed her. But what example would I be setting her if I had just allowed her to say and do what she wanted? Ryan and I are in agreement on this: the door will always be open to her, but she needs to tell the truth.

I do not regret the decisions I have made or the experiences I have been through in my life. While they have been unpleasant, they have shaped me into a stronger person.

Bitterness tried to take root in my soul, and for a while, I felt sorry for myself. I put so much faith in people who let me down, but I have come to realise that the one being that never let me down, who I spent so much time putting second and running from, was God. My hunger for acceptance and love led me on a destructive path, looking for someone I could put in the place of the mother and father I lost. Many foster parents and older people I tried to mould into these important roles came to nothing, and in the end it was God who remained loving and loyal. He is the only parent I need, and the realisation has left me a happier person, who, for the first time in life, has started to experience wholeness.

I do not worry about what others think about me or what conclusions they jump to anymore, because God tells me through his Word (Psalm 139) that I am fearfully and wonderfully made and that he knows and loves me no matter where I have been or what I have done.

I hated myself for over twenty years, ever since I was a child, and used self-harming as a way to reinforce that hatred. I am glad to say that I have not self-harmed for the last four years. God has finally set me free from its hold on me. I am not perfect and still have my down days, but the depression I suffered from an early age has gotten better. I do not think what I have been through in my life has exclusively happened to me; I know many women who have been sexually abused and their stories our similar to mine. The Bible shows us in the story of Job that life can bring one disaster after another, but we can never give up. With faith in God, we must keep pressing on and believing in him, no matter how circumstances seem. He is more than able to bring us through. I would not wish what I have been through on anybody, and if it had not been for my faith and belief in Jesus Christ, I would have probably been dead by now.

Many have wanted to see me destroyed rather than prosper into a productive and happy woman. The fact that I was abused and from the care system stacked the odds against me, and those people tried to use it as their victory card. But Jesus loves the underdog, the people who have nothing, the people society turns its nose at. Jesus came for people like me who are crushed and broken-hearted so he can fully restore them to a beauty they have never known.

I never thought life would turn out the way it has and never thought Sophia would not be a part of the great things we have started to experience this far, but I am confident God will turn around all bad things for his good. My life is just beginning, and for many years I just existed, breathing but emotionally, mentally, and spiritually dead.

God gave me a dream back in January 2009 that the house move was going to go through. I jumped up out of my sleep in excitement and told my husband that after eight months of waiting for a move to our dream area, it was going to happen. God also gave me the story in Mark 5:41 about the girl everyone thought was dead but actually was just in a deep sleep. That girl represents me, who just existed, depressed and in despair, weighed down by the guilt and shame I carried since a child. But now, in Jesus, I have slowly awoken into the woman he wants me to be, getting stronger in his Word, free from shame and guilt, fully embracing life and gaining victory.

God's plans for me are to give me a hope and a good future (Jeremiah 29:11), which thankfully includes the love of my husband and daughter Esther. I have moved to the new house we waited so long for, and I am grateful for the new beginning and know that he is going to give me double blessings for the trouble I have been through (Isaiah 61:7).

Life comes with good and bad times, with happiness and pain, and there are no guarantees that we won't face trials. And when we do face those trials, there is no formula or right or wrong way of getting through the pain we face. Nothing is in our control, and sometimes we have no choice other than to accept whatever the lesson is and use it as a personal experience to grow better and stronger. It does not matter how many mistakes you make or how many times you fall. God is a forgiving God and just asks that you come to him and ask for his help. It is not easy to dust yourself off, get up, and try again, but with his help, you can and will. I am proof of that.